The Anne Frank You Wished You Knew

Anne Frank Beyond Her Diary

Includes "The Lost Anne Frank Video"

Robert Urban M.D.
Amanda Urban

Cover Design by Amanda Urban

The Anne Frank You Wished You Knew

Anne Frank Beyond Her Diary

Includes "The Lost Anne Frank Video"

Dedication:

There Are Dreams That Cannot Be... Storms We Cannot Weather...

This book is dedicated to the following:

Anne Frank

Whose candor, honesty and tragedy reach out to teach us about ourselves and our world family.

Anne's message resonates throughout the world and continues to grow.

If Anne only knew the response to her diary - an acclaimed world class work of literature.

Anne's diary is considered to be one of the most important literary works of the 20th century!

Miep Gies

A grateful, loyal, determined and clever lifelong supporter of the Frank family and the story.

It was Miep Gies who reached down and collected the strewn pages of the scattered diary after the family was taken into custody.

Miep Gies became the needful temporary custodian of this world treasure.

In time, Miep Gies was able to give the diary to Anne Frank's father upon his return from Auschwitz Concentration Camp.

Miep Gies did much more for those in hiding.

Otto Frank

Who overcame early reservations to become the true guardian of the story and spirit of his daughter Anne.

At first critical of some of Anne's entries, Otto Frank eventually loosened his censorship to allow for the full version of the diary to be published.

Otto Frank moved to Switzerland to be with his family in 1953.

Otto Frank married Elfriede Geisinger who had been in the Auschwitz Concentration Camp.

Elfriede Geisinger was originally from Vienna. She had lost a husband and son in the concentration camps.

Otto Frank lived out his remaining years outside of Basel, Switzerland. There he devoted most of his time nurturing his daughter's story.

Otto Frank died in 1980.

You

It's up to you to take your place among the supporters of Anne Frank. Resist the Holocaust deniers for the sake of Anne Frank and so many who were silenced. Do your part.

You are connected to so many people who care about Anne Frank and the Holocaust as a tragic stain on the story of mankind.

You can keep Anne's story alive!

Tell others.

What if Anne Frank were alive today?

How would she feel about the German people?

We don't know. What we do have is what one Holocaust survivor has to say about the German people.

What if Anne Frank Were Alive Today? A Holocaust survivor answers the question: How do you feel about the German people?

2013 Holocaust survivor Rachel Rosenberg's – 1 minute answer to the question:

How do you feel about the German people?

https://www.youtube.com/watch?v=m0hsGJ_P 3rM

Check it out.

We Need Your Help - Become Part of the Story and the Book

The purpose of the book is to take the reader beyond Anne Frank's diary. For that, we need to bring new relevant information and details.

To make this book the best it can be, we want to call on our readers to send their input.

Anne Frank certainly doesn't write about all that is going on around her. She chooses her own topics for the day.

Still, there were forces around Anne that created and altered her environment. What we want to do is bring those forces and information out of the shadows while staying true to Anne's story.

Much like the line of dominos, the information we bring forward has its place.

Help us.

Do you have information that would add value to Anne's story?

Let me give you an example.

In a subsequent chapter, we discuss Anne's school situation. In reading Anne's account, she mentions a conditional school.

At first, we had the impression that the conditions related to entry requirements of sorts.

That was not the case. We found out that Anne would be going to the Jewish school because Jewish children had to attend Jewish schools through Nazi decree.

Surprise. The new information added critical relevant perspective.

As you read the book, you might have some relevant information that expands Anne's story in some way.

If that is the case, send your information to:

TheHolocaustScream@cox.net

Anne Frank's story is involved in a cyber war with forces ever willing to tear her story apart.

What better way to fight the battle than to add value and relevance to her story in your own way.

The authors can and most likely will edit and re-publish the book with small additions as they become available.

We would like to have your new material to add.

Become part of the book.

Send your information to us.

Thanks in advance,

Robert and Amanda

BONUS ADDITION #1:

Could There Be a Video of Anne Frank? Yes. The "Lost" Anne Frank Video is Found –

The Only Video of Anne Frank Known to Exist!

A precious new Anne Frank find
has surfaced at last!

The world is hungry for all things regarding Anne Frank and her diary. It was with much joy that I received the news of a "lost" Anne Frank video.

Before you check out the video, I want you to know that there are several photos of Anne Frank and her family during the years prior to Anne and her family going into hiding.

Sadly, there are no photos of Anne Frank and her family while in hiding.

Perhaps developing the pictures out in the Dutch economy would have posed too great a risk.

However, there is only one video of Anne Frank.

It was taken on the occasion of a wedding in June, 1941. Anne Frank is clearly visible in a second floor window of the building.

Holland is occupied at the time of the video. The Nazis are around. The Jews are in the open, but not for long.

Be sure to take a look. The "lost" video is 101 seconds long. Such a fleeting and precious moment in time.

Here is your link -

https://www.youtube.com/watch?v=qyFW7GMqcdI

There <u>were</u> happier times – Take a look at the "Lost" video of Anne Frank.

Rachel Rosenberg, a Holocaust survivor 2 years older than Anne, did want to read Anne's story.

Let's listen to what Rachel has to say from a unique perspective. (1 minute)

https://www.youtube.com/watch?v=qyFW7GMq cdI

BONUS ADDITION #2 - A Holocaust Survivor Reads & Reacts to Anne Frank's Diary

Rachel Rosenberg

We have a special treat for you.

I had the occasion to read Anne Frank's diary with Rachel Rosenberg. Rachel spent 6 years in 4 Nazi concentration camps with 3 years in Auschwitz Concentration Camp!

Anne Frank and Rachel both spent the late summer of 1944 in Auschwitz. According to Rachel, they never met.

Anne Frank was passing through Auschwitz on her way to what would be a succession of concentration camps.

I was surprised by Rachel Rosenberg's reaction as we read Anne's story. Rachel's reaction remains the same today.

Rachel Rosenberg's reaction is what it is.

16

Find out how a Holocaust survivor, Rachel Rosenberg, reacts to Anne Frank's circumstances and fate. Take a look at this video (3 minutes):

https://www.youtube.com/watch?v=lF_BXJz5C-M

In addition...

Rachel Rosenberg's and Anne Frank's stories have several parallels. There is a Romeo and Juliet theme in both.

Star crossed lovers

Both girls were transported in those dreadful German railcars. We don't know about Anne Frank's railcar experience. We do know how it might have been.

Rachel Rosenberg spent 13 days in a German railcar just like the one below.

Rachel remembers being packed in "like sardines." More than one hundred people were in Rachel's railcar at the start. Each prisoner was given a teaspoon of sugar per day!

Many died along the way. Their bodies were thrown out of the railcars.

Rachel witnessed the brutal death of her aunt in that railcar...because the aunt was found to have a piece of bread.

Imagine witnessing a loved one being beaten to death by starving people over a loaf of bread and you can't get away or help.

The German rail system billed the government per passenger mile. Meticulous records were kept as was the Nazi way.

After the war, many of these paper trails survived to help document the magnitude and scale of the war crimes.

German railcar circa 1940

Some of the other similarities between Rachel and Anne Frank include:

- a strong father daughter bond
- lice & typhus exposure with threat of camp obliteration by the Nazis
- an aspect of hiding but under distinctly different circumstances for each girl
- daily terror
- lost family members

Be sure to check out Rachel Rosenberg's unique perspective on Anne Frank's diary (3 minutes):

https://www.youtube.com/watch?v=lF_BXJz5C-M

Thanks for Reading Our Book

A drawing of Anne Frank

Thank you so much for reading our book.

We know that you have many tugs on your time. Then there are the many other worthy Holocaust reading and video options.

Each Holocaust story is extremely important. We have personally known more than a dozen Holocaust survivors.

Many survivors buried their experiences. Some survivors were unable to bring themselves to discuss the horrors they had endured.

They managed to keep those painful memories buried.

In many cases, children of Holocaust parents were not aware of what had happened to their parents.

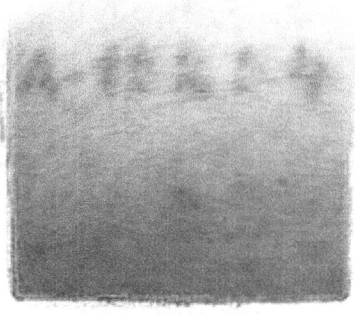

A-15254

Rachel Rosenberg's left arm tattoo acquired upon arrival at Auschwitz Concentration Camp.

Rachel Rosenberg's daughter knew something had happened. It was only when her daughter attended a college class on the Holocaust that she was able to connect that strange mark on her mother's arm to the bigger picture.

There is a group known as Second Generation of the Holocaust.

These children of Holocaust survivors have been affected in different ways. Some were unaware of the underlying cause of their situation.

These second generation children of the Holocaust consider themselves to be victims as well.

I was skeptical at first.

However, Rachel emphatically changed my opinion on the matter of second generation Holocaust victims.

In many cases, the children of the Holocaust suffered as well. There are second generation Holocaust victims.

Some of you may have just had a light go on.

Comments? Others have written us about the Second Generation of Survivors. Please email us at:

HolocaustShoah@gmail.com

Until then, enjoy the book.

Robert & Amanda Urban

Other Books by the Authors

The Holocaust Scream

The Holocaust Scream is the autobiography of Rachel Rosenberg.

Robert Urban co-authored *The Holocaust Scream* with Rachel Rosenberg, Holocaust survivor with 6 years confinement in 4 concentration camps.

The Holocaust Scream became a #1 best seller on Amazon Kindle.

The Holocaust Scream is also available in hard copy on Amazon where it may be found by searching the book's title.

Yes, there definitely was a time, a place and a Holocaust Scream.

The Holocaust Scream

Be sure to check out Rachel's compelling story after you finish this book.

Prepare to cry.

You have heard about the different and many versions of Anne Frank's diary.

Why so many versions? Let's look into it.

Which Edition Are We Talking About? - A Perspective

The edition that forms the basis for our book is, *The Definitive Edition: The Diary of a Young Girl - Anne Frank* by Anne Frank's father, Otto Frank with Miriam Pressler.

In this edition, we have the whole diary to read. Plus, as you might expect, there are some historical comments that give closure to the characters in this tragedy because....

Yes, there is more than one edition or version of Anne Frank's diary. That should not raise any questions of validity or authenticity.

There are legitimate reasons why there are multiple versions.

By the way, the Dutch version is entitled 'Het Acterhuis' or 'The Back House.'

This helps us understand that the various titles have been given by editors, authors and others close to the story.

The matter of the diary's authenticity was settled a long time ago in a Dutch court after a contentious and lengthy trial.

The Holocaust deniers and literary critics have taken their best shots at Anne Frank's diary. The diary lives!

Why the different editions?

There are several reasons.

Anne Frank started a second version of her diary when she heard a Dutch official in exile call for Dutch citizens to document their war experiences.

As a consequence, Anne went through her early entries and eliminated some trivial content. In other entries, Anne made additions but did note the additions as being separate.

In response to this call for documentation by the exiled Dutch government, Anne was given the hope that her story might a future.

Some diary editions were edited to exclude Anne's graphic discussion of her female anatomy. This may have been done because of established cultural norms.

Even today, some people believe school children should not be exposed to Anne's daring "outing" of her female anatomy.

Anne's father, Otto Frank, was moved to edit the diary to remove some of Anne's harsh criticism of her parents.

Also, Otto Frank tried to eliminate any pseudo-nyms (Anne's false assigned names) and restore all the proper names.

To that extent, Anne's father's revisions and any other alterations take away from the reality and ethos of Anne Frank's unique perspective.

In reviewing the merits of, *The Definitive Edition: The Diary of a Young Girl, Anne Frank,* we find that any adaptations and editing are fairly well hidden.

We know that Anne Frank wrote in the Dutch language. A sample of the diary in Anne's handwriting is included in the definitive edition.

The book would be very hard to read in the original based on my difficulty reading Anne Frank's sample handwriting displayed in the book.

For that reason alone, editing of some kind seems appropriate. The authors of this edition are able to impart a sense of rhythm and consistency in conveying her story from the original.

We did not sense that the authors were struggling for the meaning of the entries.

It was helpful that Anne Frank was open and clear in what she wanted to say.

There is a poem composed in tight English rhyme (December 6, 1943). We can appreciate the writer's dilemma trying to convey as much of the diary's meaning as possible while writing in another language.

In this case, some literary license is in order.

We appreciate the detailed entries. They make us feel we are reading an inclusive edition with nothing held out.

For example, there is an itemized clothing inventory (October 7, 1942). The list conveys the sense that what we are reading is authentic and complete.

Obviously, the list was important to Anne at the time.

The Definitive Edition: The Diary of a Young Girl Anne Frank portrays the teenager as openly confessing to having some guile while being refreshingly naive and vulnerable.

For the most part, Anne does not consider her guile to be a virtue.

That brings us to the discussion of Anne's comments about her female anatomy, marital innocence and teenage romance.

Anne Frank is very clear in her opinions and feelings.

We think Anne's discussion of her female anatomy adds important context and a sense of timing.

Most of us have been there. Anne was caught up in the rite of passage with regard to her sexuality.

These sexually charged entries should be included in any reading whenever available.

When putting together *The Holocaust Scream*, several people asked me to modify and even delete parts of Rachel Rosenberg's story. I was strongly opposed to any revisions.

The Holocaust produced attitudes and behaviors that were unusual in the extreme.

In the end, who are we to raise our sensitivity issues upon a true story about life and death?

Anne's account is what it is.

Other editions arose because of added editorial comments. In one instance, Anne's father, Otto Frank, is said to have published an edition in which he inserted some comments.

Then there are the "lost pages" editions. Apparently a few pages were found that qualified as being part of the diary. I believe the number of "lost pages" was five.

However, I do not know the total number of pages in the diary's full version.

Many believe that Otto Frank removed these pages. Fortunately for us, these five pages are included in this book, *The Definitive Edition: The Diary of a Young Girl - Anne Frank.*

In addition, there are the plays and other spinoffs.

We are not aware of any diary material kept back from this edition.

Through all these editions and compilations, the essence of Anne's story remains consistent, true, meaningful and potentially life-changing.

Authors Otto Frank and Miriam Pressler do mankind a service by bringing to us, in a very readable, comprehensive and lasting edition, *The Definitive Edition: The Diary of a Young Girl - Anne Frank.*

It is this edition that forms the foundation for our book, *The Anne Frank You Wished You Knew.*

A book found lying on a floor. What's the problem? Why the considerable resistance to the book?

Not everyone liked the diary of Anne Frank. So...

What About Those Many Struggles the Diary Has Had to Endure?

You may have a general sense about the story of Anne Frank. That's the story narrative. But were you aware that the diary had to survive a series of existential threats?

It was Miep Gies, a secretary, worker and one of the four outsiders who knew about those in hiding, who discovered the diary on the floor of the Annex.

On her own initiative, Miep Gies kept the diary for Otto Frank.

Miep Gies gave the diary to Otto Frank upon his return to Amsterdam shortly after World War II had ended. Miep Gies stated she had not read the diary. Imagine.

Otto Frank kept the diary until the early 1950s when he decided to have it published. In preparation for the first publication, Otto Frank purged about a third of the diary. The purged material has been included in:

The Definitive Edition: The Diary Of A Young Girl - Anne Frank

Indeed, Anne Frank revised her original entries after deciding to make the diary available to the public after the war. Anne used pseudonyms or literary aliases in her revised edition.

Otto Frank eventually restored the original names to the diary.

The diary started slowly on the world scene. Then came the wholesale attacks from many groups and individuals questioning the authenticity of the diary.

A Dutch commission was convened to sort things out. In time, the commission ruled in favor of the diary's authenticity.

Today, all editions have been accepted as conveying the same essence, the tragic struggles of a young girl living under life and death circumstances.

Anne's diary is considered to be one of the 20th century's great pieces of literature.

Still, there are detractors, critics and naysayers.

Some people raised questions about the authenticity of the book based on their perceptions of literary style, Otto Frank's business identity, so-called anachronisms (a.k.a. material that somehow conflicts with the historical period and events) etc.

I have no comments regarding these issues. In the end, you decide.

The judges who do matter have made their decision. All over the world, people have read and accepted Anne Frank's story as being authentic.

Keep in mind that there is tension associated with Anne Frank. It is not just her diary that moves people in strong emotional ways.

The times and the broad range of human behavior captivate us and will do so for all time.

Anne's story is truly evergreen as is this discussion.

EVERGREEN MEANS

ALIVE TOMORROW

The Anne Frank You Wished You Knew is Evergreen as well - Spread the word

This book strives to add context and perspective to Anne Frank's diary to help the interested reader. There is much to be said about Anne Frank.

Note:

Otto Frank was asked about the source of the diary's power and popularity. He said that the diary covered so many areas of life and while doing so, each reader is moved or emotionally connected to Anne and the situations she faced.

For some, these connections can be visceral, even disturbing.

There is something in the diary for everyone, even detractors. If you think about it, you can't really say that about a lot of books.

Simon Wiesenthal praised the book for raising the awareness of the Holocaust which the diary certainly does.

Who was Simon Wiesenthal (1908-2005)?

At the end of World War II, many Nazis were still living in freedom and trying to hide their past.

Simon Wiesenthal was a Holocaust death camp survivor. Simon Wiesenthal dedicated the rest of his life to documenting the crimes of the Holocaust and hunting down the perpetrators still at large.

"When history looks back," Wiesenthal explained, "I want people to know the Nazis weren't able to kill millions of people and get away with it."

His life's work stands as a reminder of the depths of the Holocaust depravity and warns future generation to be diligent. Individuals are to be accountable for their actions.

Simon Wiesenthal was founder and head of the Jewish Documentation Center in Vienna.

Often with the cooperation of the Israeli, Austrian, former West German and other governments, the Center searched out nearly 1,100 Nazi war criminals, many of whom had been prominent Nazis.

Simon Wiesenthal made a remarkable comparison when he noted the Diary of Anne Frank raised more widespread awareness of the Holocaust than the Nuremberg trials!

Simon Wiesenthal went on to say that, "People identified with this child. This was my family, like your family and so you could understand this."

We hope this book takes you deep into the intricacies of the Anne Frank tragedy leaving you with a better perspective of what took place and why.

Take others to the light. Keep the flame alive. Tell others about the book.

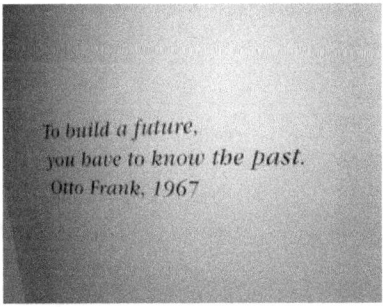

To build a future,
you have to know the past.
Otto Frank, 1967

Remember: Anne Frank is evergreen. So is this book.

As we shall see, the Frank family's situation in Holland has a historical foundation.

Holland had become a haven and culture for political and religious dissenters. Opposing that were the more prevalent negative cultures, which had persecuted the Jews for centuries...

1492, Marranos and Spain - Important Anne Frank Background Issues You Should Know

When Anne Frank begins her diary, she does not mention the troubles that surround her. The Franks are in a gathering storm of troubles. They are on the run and have been for some time.

To help understand the difficulties that threaten the Franks and other European Jews, let us go back in time to....

In 1492, Queen Isabel and King Ferdinand of Spain marry and unite to form the Kingdom of Spain.

It had been a long unification struggle for the Spaniards. There was an ongoing war of about 700 years between the Christian and Muslim factions. Each faction wanted to control the Spanish peninsula.

Once in power, the Spanish monarchs gave Christopher Columbus the backing and blessing to seek new worlds.

We know how that story unfolds with the discovery of the Americas by Spanish forces.

However, in the same year that Columbus set sail for the Indies, the Spanish monarchs issued a decree that forced all Spanish Jews to convert to Christianity, leave the country or be killed.

The so called Edict of Expulsion was the latest in the struggle between Catholic and Jewish forces in Spain.

The Edict was not the first attempt by Spanish forces to force Christian baptism and behavior upon the Jews.

Many Spanish Jews chose to leave Spain. The Jews going into exile were called Marranos.

But where could the Marranos go?

As it turned out, the Marranos had some choices.

Some Marranos had money and more importantly, skills, education, cache with others and connections.

Some of these Jewish exiles were like mobile enterprise centers.

Many of these Spanish Jews could take their skills to places where they were in demand. Of course, not all the Marranos were that mobile and fortunate.

The Marranos were openly encouraged to settle in several places in the eastern Mediterranean. However, that part of the world was largely under the control of Muslim forces.

It is said that the Muslim Sultan of the Ottoman Empire openly chided King Ferdinand of Spain for enriching the Sultan's lands at the expense of the Spanish kingdom.

In this case, Spain's considerable economic losses were the Ottoman Empire's gain.

Many Marranos chose to settle in other parts of Western Europe. Poland was a relative haven for Jews although they settled in Poland with the mixed and shifting blessings of the Polish authorities and citizenry.

In most places, the Jews were tolerated although their fortunes tended to ebb and flow.

What is now Holland had become a reluctant province of the Spanish empire.

Over time, Holland developed a sailing economy, independence from Spain and a culture of genuine religious tolerance.

The Dutch culture of tolerance was to play itself out in the middle of the 20th century and benefit the Franks.

During World War 2, some Jews could hide in Holland. No Jew could hide in Poland according to Rachel Rosenberg.

Nothing could fully prepare World Jewry for the horror to come. There had been Nazi threats and writings. Were these threats just propaganda?

Not to one person.

Adolph Hitler's autobiography, Mein Kampf (My Struggle), had been clear in revealing Hitler's intent to bring about the annihilation of the Jews. Mein Kampf was published in 1925.

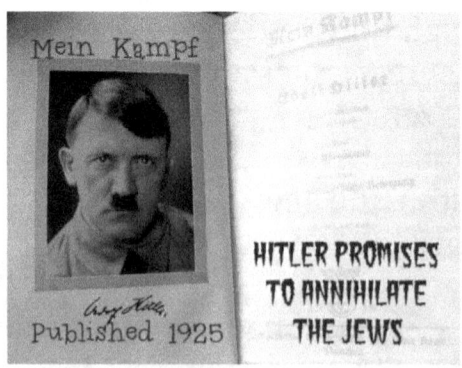

Mein Kampf - My Struggle was written while Hitler was in prison for trying to overthrow the German government

Few people other than the Nazis thought Hitler would carry through on his threat to totally annihilate the Jews.

Most believed Hitler and the Nazis were exaggerating for political gain.

That was the collective mindset of most observers including many of the Germans. They were wrong.

This brings us to 1933 when the Nazi juggernaut became entrenched in German politics.

Would Hitler do what he said he would do to the Jews? The Frank family believed Hitler would act on his threats to destroy the Jews.

In time, the Nazis would become like a plague on all mankind.

This description was given to me by another Holocaust survivor who wrote in response to reading our book, *The Holocaust Scream.*

I thought it appropriate. The Nazis as a plague on mankind stuck with me.

How Did the Great Depression Contribute To The Holocaust?

What if you could leave Germany? The Germans did their best to insure that those leaving were completely impoverished as soon as they tried to leave.

In 1933, the Great Depression was in full force. No country looked forward to a mass influx of penniless people seeking work. Every country was already overrun with its own unemployed citizens.

The economy was a big factor. Some people believe the Great Depression was the main reason Hitler came out of nowhere to assume political power in Germany.

In her book, *The Holocaust Scream*, Rachel Rosenberg states that no Pole would hide a Jew. That was under Nazi occupation of Poland where it would mean death to any Pole hiding a Jew.

On the other hand, Holland was receptive to Jews seeking refuge, but only for a while. As the years passed, more Jews sought refuge in Holland.

The influx of Jews put pressure on the Dutch to limit the number of refugees.

In 1938, there was an Evian Conference held in France to discuss the problem of the Jewish exiles and possible places of refuge.

Only Holland and Denmark would agree to let in more Jews. The other countries would not raise their immigration quotas. This included the United States.

We can only guess as to how Otto Frank circumvented the economic issues.

First of all, Otto Frank was proactive. He moved his family early in an attempt to avoid Nazi persecution. The Franks had relatives in Switzerland and had vacationed there.

Anne makes no mention of Switzerland although she would have been very young at the time her family visited Switzerland.

It appears that Switzerland was not a topic of discussion among the adults during their years in hiding.

In the end, Switzerland managed to escape Nazi occupation. Hitler considered invading Switzerland but thought the mountainous terrain and armed populace would be too difficult to overcome.

Besides, Hitler needed his forces elsewhere once the fighting started.

Otto Frank must have had some capital or was able to transfer some capital to Holland. In any event, he had economic connections which served him well.

Otto Frank became an employer in Holland. His company produced jams and jellies.

In her diary, Anne Frank talks about food monotony and shortages, but never a shortage of means to pay for provisions.

That leads us to conclude that Otto Frank chose Holland because he could make it work.

Otto Frank's daughter Anne was not privy to the details of her father's economic connections other than the fact that Otto Frank was partnered with Hermann Van Pels (Van Daan), head of the other family in hiding.

Anne makes several references to prices on the inevitable black market. Provisions could be had, for a price.

Anne notes prices were going up.

It wasn't so much that Holland was a great place to live. Rather, the problem at first for the Franks lay within Germany.

That takes us back to Germany....

Background Question: Why Were the Franks Living in Holland?

In 1933, approximately 450,000 Jews lived in Germany. Hitler and the Nazis came into power in 1933.

Immediately, Some Jews, including the Franks, began to leave Germany.

In the first year or so, about 50,000 Jews left Germany as these Jews acted to stay ahead of the Nazi's inevitable plan to destroy Jews everywhere.

If over 10% of the German Jews left in the first year of Nazi ascendency, doesn't that speak volumes.

There was a depression everywhere. It could not have been easy to move. Still... there were those threats.

Otto Frank and his family moved to Amsterdam. The maternal grandmother was unable to accompany the others. There were later attempts to get the grandmother out but to no avail.

Many people within the German Jewish community believed the Franks and other Jews were overreacting to the danger. The Nazis or really Hitler's ranting against the Jews was perceived as mostly talk.

Were the Franks and others panicking? Germans were Germans, right? Cultured and all that.

In Poland, Rachel Rosenberg's mother told her the Germans were "cultured." The Germans would not be that bad. Rachel's mother was wrong.

This perspective immediately cost Rachel Rosenberg's mother her life along with Rachel's youngest brother. The Nazis were out to annihilate the Jews everywhere.

Like a frog in water as the temperature rises, the unrelenting heat was turned on the remaining Jews in Germany.

Decree after decree began to progressively endanger those Jews who remained in Germany.

For example, the Nuremberg Laws which forbade, among many things, interracial marriage.

Later on, we discuss how the Nuremberg Laws forbidding interracial marriage would impact one of our couples.

Also, Jewish medical professionals were not allow to practice.

By the time of Kristallnact in 1938, every Jew living in Germany knew their situation was only going to get worse.

Kristallnacht or the Night of Broken Glass, was the day when rampaging German mobs attacked Jews, Jewish businesses and synagogues.

November 9th, 1938, Kristallnacht or Crystal Night - The Night of Broken Glass.

There was no place in the Nazi's Third Reich for Jews!

Getting out of Germany became the fervent desire of just about every remaining Jew in Germany.

By 1938, some 150,000 Jews had left Germany, 300,000 Jews remained.

By then, it had become much harder for Jews to leave Germany, much harder. In this regard, the Frank family was fortunate to have left when they did in 1933.

The Franks would have some quality time together. And yet...

Other Jews were now trapped inside Germany

Was Anne Frank really a German?? So, the burning question is .....

Question #1 - Where was Anne Frank Born?

We know that Anne Frank and her family went into hiding in Amsterdam, Holland.

Where was Anne Frank born?

Your choices are:

1. Wolinow, Poland.

2. Amsterdam, Holland.

3. Cologne, Germany.

4. Frankfurt, Germany.

Answer to Question #1 - Where was Anne Frank Born?

1933: "Germans
Defend yourselves
Don't buy from the Jews"

4. Frankfurt, Germany.

Discussion:

Anne Frank was born in Frankfurt, Germany.

Her full name is Annelies Marie Frank. Her birthdate is listed as June 12, 1929.

Anne received her diary as a birthday gift on June 12, 1942. The gift was a red covered book or journal. Anne was expecting the diary. Anne had pointed the diary out to one of her parents.

Anne had the diary in her possession about one month before she went into hiding.

"Because we were Jewish." is the reason Anne gave as to why the Frank family left Germany in 1933.

Anne Frank's father, Otto, became managing director of the Opetka Company in Amsterdam.

The Opetka Company manufactured jellies and jams. These food connections would prove useful.

It is interesting that Anne Frank's maternal grandmother was named Rosa Hollander. The surname suggests a historical connection with Holland.

The fort of the Franks or Frankfurt, was the starting point for the Frank family.

The Franks were an ancient migrating tribe that eventually settled in France, giving the country its name. In their tribal wanderings, the Franks set up a fortress at Frankfurt.

Ironically, Frank means free man.

June 12, 1942

Anne was not a Dutch citizen.

April 11, 1944

Doing the Unthinkable - Split Up the Family?

Could they, would they split up?

Anne Frank's father, Otto, was on top of things as much as he could be.

Otto Frank tried to obtain U.S. visas for his immediate family just before they went into hiding in 1942. Holland was occupied by the Nazis at that time.

By then, the task of obtaining visas for German Jews to go anywhere was extremely difficult. Allied and Axis countries had progressively tightened immigration policies.

Apparently money was a consideration as Otto Frank sent desperate letters to friends and family in the U.S. pleading for help with immigration expenses.

In letters that were to come to light after many years, Otto Frank writes poignantly and in a way that barely conceals his desperation,

"I would not ask if conditions here would not force me to do all I can in time to be able to avoid worse...

It is for the sake of the children mainly that we have to care for. Our own fate is of less importance."

Otto Frank was writing to his college friend Nathan Straus in April, 1941.

Otto Frank was trying to get his immediate family of four plus his mother-in-law, Rosa Hollander, to safety in Cuba or the United States.

Anne's father sensed that war was imminent. Otto Frank's attempt to attain these "late" visas began in April 30, 1941 and ceased on December 11, 1941, when Hitler unilaterally declared war on the United States.

The bombing of Pearl Harbor by the Japanese closed the door for the Franks living in Holland. Japan was an ally of Germany. Germany declared war on the U.S. to support its ally.

By then, nearly 300,000 people were on a waiting list for U.S. immigration visas. Most of those on the list were desperate Jews like the Franks. Jews now wanted to leave Europe.

In a classic Catch 22 situation, the Franks had living relatives in Germany. Under U.S. immigration policy at the time, the Frank family was unable to immigrate straight to the U.S. because of this rule.

Of course, the Franks would have to first go back to Germany to enjoy the questionable benefits of reverse immigration.

Not likely. The Germans would be waiting.

For their part, the Americans did not want to get involved in European politics. President Roosevelt and other politicos faced a strong pacifist movement. Most of these pacifists embraced isolationism.

Memories of World War I had created the pacifist movement and isolationism. The pacifists did not want the United States to again try to solve Europe's problems.

The pacifists believe the European Jews' problems needed to stay in Europe. Let the Europeans solve their own problems.

While in college, I met a woman who had been head of the student pacifist movement in the same college before the United States entered World War II.

The woman told me the pacifists were numerous, strong, vibrant, politically active and involved.

I asked her what happened to the pacifists.

She replied, "After Pearl Harbor, there were no pacifists."

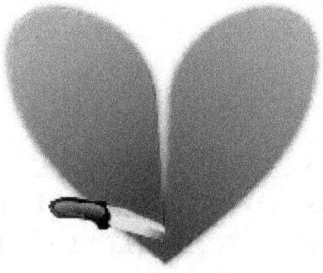

Otto Frank and his wife Edith pondered the unthinkable, splitting the family.

Otto writes,

"I know that it will be impossible for us all to leave even if most of the money is refundable, but **Edith urges me to leave alone or with the children.**"

In 1941, Otto Frank managed to secure a single visa to Cuba for himself. The visa was canceled in

December 1941, after the Germans declared war on the U.S.
The Frank family went into hiding seven months later.

By then, the Franks were trapped inside Holland. Otto Frank had sensed what was coming. Anne's father was powerless to get out from under the Nazis.

Their fate was sealed.

At this time, Anne was making entries into her diary. Her father's concerns were kept from her.

Let us pick up Anne as the diary begins.....

Question #2 - Anne Frank Wrote that She Started Her Book Because...

Your choices are:

1. She wanted to remember details she would otherwise forget.

2. The Dutch government in exile broadcast pleas for its citizens to document their experiences.

3. No one took her seriously. The book would be a way of remembering these important personal times.

4. She needed a friend.

Answer to Question #2 - Anne Frank Wrote that She Started Her Book Because..

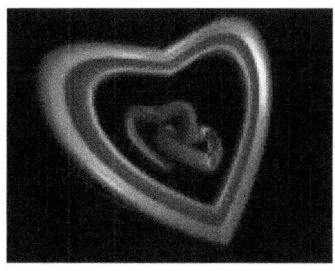

A friend

4. She needed a friend.

Anne Frank was introspective. She later wrote that she could detach herself and look upon her inner self as if that part was a separate person.

Anne saw her diary as a "long awaited friend."

Anne felt she could not get close to people. She could not confide with anyone and that was not likely to change.

It was after Anne had her diary and was in hiding that she heeded the advice broadcast by the Dutch government in exile encouraging Dutch citizens to document the occupation by the Nazis.

At this time, Anne felt compelled to edit some of her original entries.

June 20, 1942

Question #3 - What Event Caused the Franks to Go Into Hiding?

? What danger

A call up notice was an order issued to an individual to report to a collection facility.

Those who reported were to be deported to the East. The deportees vanished and were never heard from again. Little else was known about the process at that time.

Your choices are:

1. Mr. Van Daan, Anne's father's Jewish business partner and close friend, received an SS call up notice.

2. Anne's older sister Margot received an SS call up notice.

3. Anne's father, Otto Frank, received an SS call up notice.

4. Anne Frank received an SS call up notice.

So, who got the dreaded call up notice?

Answer to Question 3 - What Event Caused the Franks to Go Into Hiding?

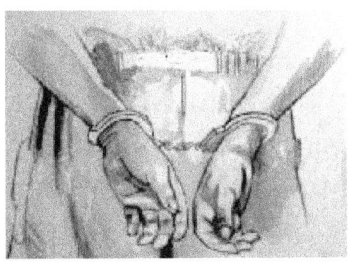

2. Anne's older sister Margot received an SS call up notice.

Discussion:

At first, Anne believed the call up notice was for her father. In fact, the call up notice was for Anne's sister, Margot. That situation was clarified the same day.

The Franks fallback position was to go into hiding. They had planned and set aside provisions for going into hiding.

On the day of the call up notice, the Franks immediately went into hiding along with the Van Daans (Van Pels), the family of Otto Frank's business partner.

Remember, Otto Frank was trying to obtain visas to the U.S. or Cuba as recently as seven months earlier.

July 8, 1942

The wheels had not come off. However, it was a tipping point. Everything had changed. Things were not going to be the same ever again.

A tipping point of no return

The Franks had to act fast.

A call up notice meant the person was to report to the Nazis. Then that person disappeared. That part was clear.

Question #4 - How Old Was Anne Frank When She Went into Hiding?

Growing up

Your choices are:

1. 12 years old

2. 13 years old

3. 14 years old

4. 15 years old

Answer to Question #4 - How Old Was Anne Frank When She Went Into Hiding?

Hiding in plain sight

2. 13 years old

Anne Frank was the youngest of the eight people who hid in the Annex. The others include Anne's three family members, the three Van Daans and eventually Mr. Dussel.

The Franks and Van Daans had prepared for this moment. They all realized that Margot's call up was terrible in all its implications.

There could be no turning back.

Question #5 - Where Was the Hiding Place?

Where could any Jew hide in Holland?

Where was the hiding place?

Your choices are:

1. They used 2 hiding places. They had to move once because of a sudden threat.

2. They hid above the ground floor of her father's business establishment.

3. They hid in the basement of her father's warehouse.

4. They hid in the isolated storage facility on the roof of her father's warehouse.

Answer to Question #5 - Where Was the Hiding Place?

The location of the Secret Annex - 263 Prinsengracht Amsterdam, Holland

2. They hid above the ground floor of her father's business establishment.

The Annex at the back of the business establishment measured 75 square meters. Not much. 15 x 25 feet would be the rough equivalent.

You can get at glimpse of the inside of the Annex in 3D at:

http://www.annefrank.org/en/Subsites/Home/

After some advance planning by her parents and with the help of several of her father's employees, Anne's parents managed to cache some supplies in anticipation of hiding from the Germans and their Dutch collaborators.

The ground floor of the business establishment was very much used as an active business. Those in hiding had to take this into account by remaining very quiet during business hours.

Although Otto Frank had his business located at the above address, he did not own the building.

OTTO FRANK WAS AN IMPORTER OF ...S & FRUIT

FOOD SOURCES

Question #6 - Anne Frank Changed Her Target Audience Because...

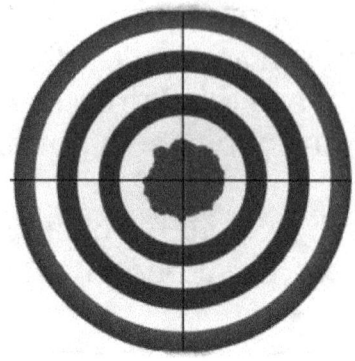

People have tried to add, modify, oppose or otherwise edit Anne Frank's diary for a lot of reasons.

While in the process of writing her diary, Anne Frank discusses her audience from her point of view. Anne believed that in the future ....

Your choices are:

1. Anne believed her diary would not be controversial.

2. Anne recognized her honest sexual discussions would offend some people.

3. Anne recognized she did not always treat her parents with respect as she should.

4. Anne realized she might be writing her diary for posterity and therefore she must edit it.

Answer to Question #6 - Anne Frank Changed Her Target Audience Because...

Could it be? How far could the diary go?

4. Anne realized she might be writing her diary for posterity and therefore she must edit it.

Discussion:

While hiding, it was the Frank family's custom to listen to radio broadcasts that were forbidden by the German authorities and their Dutch collaborators.

On one occasion, the Dutch authorities in exile called for citizens to document what was happening to the Dutch people, especially their hardships.

Anne decided she would keep her diary with this in mind.

Upon reflection, Anne thought she should edit her diary. Anne changed some entries.

We can see this self-imposed editing starting with the first entry.

Because of Anne's editing actions, she produced both version A, representing the diary without Anne's later editing and version B, which includes the post editing entries and is therefore more complete.

To be sure, Anne did not start another diary.

Question #7 - The Diary of Anne Frank Covers What Time Period?

The diary of Anne Frank covers the period?

Your choices are:

1. June 12, 1938 through August 1, 1944.

2. June 12, 1940 thru August 1, 1944.

3. June 12, 1942 thru August 1, 1944.

4. Accept for the beginning entry and noting some important events, Anne did not use dates.

In the next chapter, remember that political mantra is what we refer to as spin.

Let's follow Hitler's propaganda spin in the next chapter...

Answer to Question #7 - The Diary of Anne Frank Covers What Time Period?

Karma: What goes around comes around

3. June 12, 1942 thru August 1, 1944.

Discussion:

The group was discovered and taken away 3 days after the last entry in Anne's diary.

The time span of the diary is clear. The book was begun at a time near the high watermark of the German Third Reich - summer of 1942.

Every entry has a date.

In 1942, Europe was already mostly conquered by the Germans. German armies were racing across Russia and seemed unstoppable.

Hitler's war mantra to the German people had been a fast and successful war, The Blitzkrieg or Lightning War.

Hitler's war mantra was about to change.

The massive and encouraging German defeat at Stalingrad (central Russia) was six months in the future when Anne began her diary.

The Russians had been collecting themselves for a push back against the German forces.

In the fall of 1942, Anne mentions what has now become the famous Battle of Stalingrad.

Stalingrad was in south central Russia. The city carried Stalin's name. Therefore, Hitler wanted to conquer Stalingrad.

The Russian dictator Josef Stalin did not want Stalingrad to surrender because it carried his name. Otherwise, the city had no military importance!

German soldiers surrendering at Stalingrad wearing light winter clothing as temperatures at times reached 40 below zero.

Stalingrad winter 1942 - Many German soldiers froze to death!

Anne's entries about the battle of Stalingrad were not extensive. As early as November of 1942, she began expressing the thought that the fall of Stalingrad was imminent.

Hitler would not pull back his troops as they were about to be surrounded at Stalingrad. Hitler gave consistent stand and fight orders to his soldiers at Stalingrad. It was madness.

Stalingrad capitulated in late January of 1943. The pending fall of Stalingrad must have raised the spirits for anyone in hiding and those feeling the pressure of the Nazi boots.

In all, 300,000 German troops perished at Stalingrad. Their demise was aided by a very harsh winter. Most of the German soldiers at Stalingrad froze to death!

Karma had come around.

Adolph Hitler made only 2 major public appearances after the fall of Stalingrad. Unfortunately, the fighting continued for almost 3 more years.

After the defeat of the German army at Stalingrad, the Nazis changed their mantra or propaganda spin. Instead of a fast and successful war, the German people were told and asked to participate in Totaler Krieg or Total War.

In Total War, German defeats like Stalingrad, might come. In the end the Germans would somehow prevail as a matter of will and unity.

Why is this important? The Nazis prolonged the fighting beyond the point of any hope of victory.

Because the Nazis were willing and able to prolong the war, people hiding from the Nazis continued to be at risk of being discovered.

The maniacal prolongation of the war would eventually impact the Frank family.

I told Rachel Rosenberg about the fall of Stalingrad. I told her it was possible that some of the Nazi troops who terrorized her in Poland met their frozen fate at Stalingrad.

Rachel only said, "Good."

I believe many other victims of Nazi persecution felt the same way.

The third mantra unfolds near the end of the fighting in 1945 and would deliberately direct cruelty toward the Germans...

It is called The Nero Option after 1st century Roman emperor Nero.

The answer and discussion is in chapter 40. Be sure to check it out.

The third mantra is relevant to Anne Frank.

Question #8 - What Was the Occasion Which Led to Anne's Getting Her Diary?

Anne's diary was initially:

Your choices are:

1. a birthday present which Anne Frank knew about in advance.

2. a surprise birthday present.

3. a ledger book gift with blank pages converted into a diary.

4. a diary purchased for her sister and now handed down to Anne.

In those days, keeping a diary was the equivalent of a Facebook or Twitter presence.

Anne was eager to get started.

It was a happy time of sorts. Anne had no idea of how bad it could become, but someone did....

Answer to Question #8 - What Was the Occasion Which Led to Anne's Getting Her Diary?

1. a birthday present which Anne Frank knew about in advance.

Discussion:

On June 12, 1942, Anne Frank received a diary as a birthday present. She knew about the diary in advance and was still excited to get it. Anne made her first entry into the diary on her birthday.

Anne Frank was not in hiding when she received the diary.

"I'll begin from the moment I got you, the moment I saw you lying on the table among my other birthday presents. (I went along when you were bought but that doesn't count.)"

June 12, 1942

Question # 9 - What Name Did Anne Frank Give Her Diary?

Who am I?

Right away, Anne gave her diary a name. What name did Anne give her diary?

Your choices are:

1. Dee

2. Kitty

3. Anna

4. Friend

Answer to Question # 9 - What Name Did Anne Frank Give Her Diary?

Call me Kitty

Kitty

Discussion:

Within two months of starting her diary, she refers to the diary as Kitty. The reason she chose Kitty is unknown.

Anne consistently referred to the diary as Kitty.

September 28, 1942 (as an addition to an earlier entry).

Question # 10 - How Did Anne Respond to the Punitive "Chatterbox" Extra Homework Assignment?

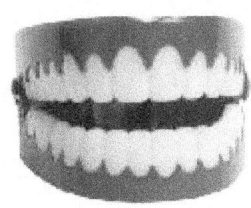

Just before going into hiding, Anne's math teacher, Mr. Keesing, found fault with Anne because she talked a lot. As a result, Mr. Keesing gave Anne extra homework.

Anne was required to write an essay titled, "A Chatterbox." In her response, Anne wanted to defend herself.

Her defense was -

Your choices are:

1. I have many friends who need to talk to me about important things.

2. Mathematics is not very verbal. The class is long. We eventually begin to talk among ourselves.

3. Talking is a female trait. My mom talks a lot....there is not much you can do about inherited traits.

4. My math is only average. In frustration, my mind wanders and I start to talk. I am good at talking, not math.

Answer to Question # 10 - How Did Anne Respond to the Punitive "Chatterbox" Extra Homework Assignment?

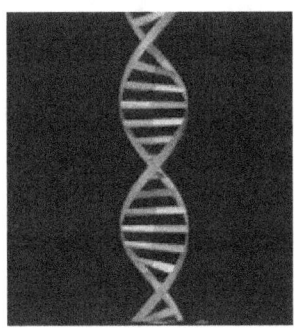

It's in the genes

3. "Talking is a female trait. My mom talks a lot....there is not much you can do about inherited traits."

Discussion:

Anne's response was correct for her gender. Research 60 years later would show that females have five brain centers for language. Males have 2 brain centers for language.

Women have more brain anatomy available for talking.

Women are more talkative and it is a way they use their brains. Expect women to talk.

Anne had a point.

June 21, 1942

Question #11 - How Good Was Anne as a Student?

How good were Anne Frank's grades?

Your choices are:

1. Anne received average grades. She thought girls could not go far outside the home.

2. Anne had average grades which greatly disappointed her parents.

3. Anne did not report her grades in the diary. Anne did make comments about her above average grades.

4. Anne was not as smart as her sister, Margot, but did not want to be a poor student.

Answer to Question #11 - How Good Was Anne as a Student?

Good grades - yes or no?

4. Anne was not as smart as her sister Margot, but did not want to be a poor student.

Discussion:

According to Anne, her parents were not concerned about her grades. Anne did think that knowing about things was important.

In one entry, Anne listed her grades. This was before the Frank family went into hiding.

"My report card wasn't too bad. I got one D, one C- in algebra, all the rest B's, except for two B+'s and 2 B-'s."

Anne did "qualify" for placement in a Jewish School. Her placement was conditional.

Jewish children had to attend Jewish schools. It is clear that as Anne writes about her placement, she does not seem to be aware of the fact that it is conditional upon her being Jewish.

There were other Jewish restrictions.

There was a curfew. Jews had to be off the street by 8:00 p.m. Also, the Jews could not ride the streetcars.

July 5, 1942

Question #12 - How Many People Went Into Hiding?

And the number is...

Initially, how many people went into hiding? That number eventually grew to what number?

Your choices are:

1. At first, 7 people went into the Annex. One was added weeks later. Total = 8.

2. 8 people were in the initial group. There were no additions. Total = 8

3. Initially, 5 people went into hiding and were joined by 3 others weeks later. Total = 8

4. Initially, 10 people went into hiding. 2 people left the group & were not replaced. Total = 8

Want to preview the answer in detail?

How about a video that shows the roster of those that went into hiding?

http://www.annefrank.org/en/Subsites/Home/

For more discussion...

Answer to Question #12 - How Many People Went Into Hiding?

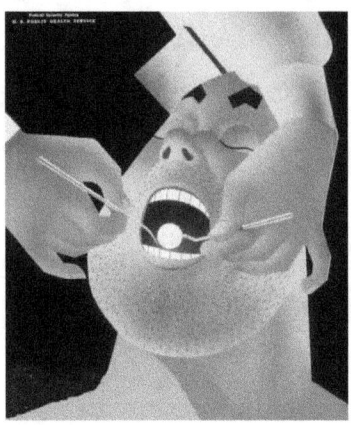

1. At first, 7 people went into the Annex. One was added weeks later - a total of 8.

Discussion:

The group agreed to add a dentist, Mr. Dussel, about 5 months after the group went into hiding.

None of the original 7 opposed the addition of an eighth resident in the Annex.

The original seven in hiding had sympathy for those on the outside who had no place to hide. Anne's entry on this matter was rather matter of fact.

November 10, 1942

Question #13 – The Group Decided to Speak in Which Language?

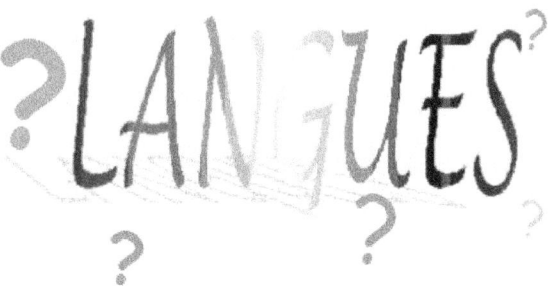

The group agreed that in addition to speaking softly, they would speak in which language?

Your choices are:

1. German. Anne's father could not understand or communicate in the Dutch language.

2. No German.

3. Yiddish.

4. German but with reluctance. All those in hiding had lived in Germany. They all understood German.

The group was about to make a principled stand, though small.

Perhaps they wanted a minor victory in their struggles against the Nazis.

Answer to Question #13 – The Group Decided to Speak in Which Language?

German free zone!

2. No German.

Discussion:

"only the language of civilized people may be spoken."

They spoke in the Dutch language.

November 17, 1942

Question #14 - Why Was Mr. Dussel Added to the Group?

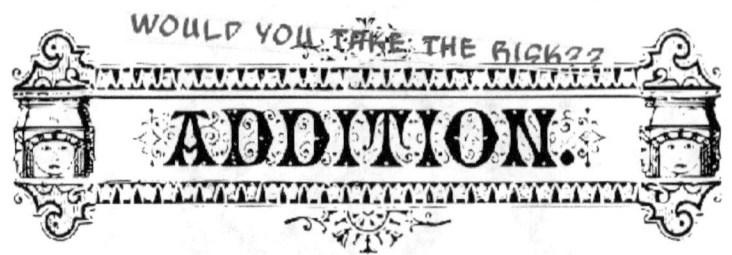

Would you take the risk?

Why was Mr. Dussel added to the group?

Your choices are:

1. Mr. Dussel was Otto Frank's best friend.

2. Mr. Dussel was well-connected and could get food and other supplies.

3. Mr. Dussel was offered a place out of kindness. The group realized they had room for one more.

4. Mr. Dussel was the one outsider who knew about the annex & might crack under pressure.

Answer to Question #14 - Why Was Mr. Dussel Added to the Group?

An act of kindness or Jewish mitzvah

3. Mr. Dussel was offered a place out of kindness. The group realized they had room for one more.

It was a Jewish good deed or mitzvah.

Discussion:

As incredible as it seems, with all the stress they were going through, the group decided that the Jews on the outside had it much worse.

Therefore, the group decided they had room for one more and added Mr. Dussel, a dentist. It was an act of kindness, a mitzvah.

Could you even imagine what you might do?

So... What would you do?

Question #15 - What Did Anne Think Happened to Those Called Up by the Nazis?

As the roundup of the Jews continued, through a window looking onto a street, Anne could see groups of people being led off at night.

Anne thought that these people were most likely going to:

Your choices are:

1. be sent to crowded collection centers with terrible living conditions.

2. be sent to the East to be resettled.

3. Who could be sure of their destination? There were so many conflicting rumors.

4. be sent to their deaths.

Answer to Question #15 - What Did Anne Think Happened to Those Called Up by the Nazis?

Behind every lying Nazi smile was the reality of death

4. be sent to their deaths.

Discussion:

"...all are marched to their deaths."

In her diary, Anne Frank does not anticipate future readers doubting the reality of her experience. Anne does believe the information in her diary may be available to future readers.

Such statements as, "How could anyone doubt?" or "What more do I have to say to convince you?" and other similar statements are often made by people who have been challenged by or anticipate some push back to their stated positions or interpretation of the facts.

Anne Frank makes no such statements.

This takes on a degree of importance when it comes to responding to Holocaust deniers. One position the deniers take is to doubt that mass gassing was used. Rather, they offer medical causes for the majority of deaths.

Really?

Let's not debate the forensic evidence found in the piles of corpses who have been starved to an extreme. Anne knew that those being taken away are worse off than those able to hide.

For Anne and many others, "all were marched to their deaths." That's the bottom line.

For those reading this book now and in the future, remember that Anne Frank is a witness against Holocaust denial by what she wrote, how she wrote it and by what she did not write.

November 19, 1942

Anne Frank was aware of the Gestapo. She mentions them by name.

The word Gestapo is a confluence of the German words Geheime Staats Polizei or Home State Police.

In her diary, Anne Frank announces the terrible news that many of their friends and acquaintances are being taken away in large numbers.

Anne connects the Gestapo to this destruction. As I read this notice from Anne's diary, I asked Rachel Rosenberg if she could relate to this part of Anne's story about the Gestapo.

Rachel said, "I haven't heard the word Gestapo in a long time."

Rachel went on to say that whenever the Gestapo came, "There was death. We would all be shaking when the knew the Gestapo were present. Some of us were going to die that day.

The Gestapo did not kill on the spot, they would lead the people off."

I asked Rachel if reading Anne Frank's diary caused her problems. She said, "No, I like to find out what others went through. I like reading the book. I slept well and feel okay."

Rachel went back to the Gestapo. "The Gestapo were special police. They were everywhere. They were much worse than the SS (special army units-rtu). The Gestapo had uniforms that were different from the SS. I think they were brown."

Rachel continued, "The Gestapo looked so terrible in their uniforms and boots. They had death signs on their shoulders and hats."

Nazi SS Totenkopf or Death's Head soldier's cap, 1934–45 Sowing & Reaping

The Gestapo were under the administration of the SS. Both groups were fiercely loyal to Hitler. The Gestapo followed Hitler's orders literally to the end of the war.

The Gestapo worked more in the administrative shadows and not so much on the battlefront.

In the last days of the war, when the Germans were about to be utterly defeated, the Gestapo went about killing Germans who the Gestapo suspected were not doing enough for the cause.

By that time, the lost cause was reduced to fighting to the bitter end.

Chapter 40 discusses Hitler's Nero Option.

The Gestapo were especially looking for military deserters who were hanged on the spot to warn others.

If you are watching a war movie and a long dark car pulls up and several men in long leather coats get out, it is most likely the Gestapo. No one looked forward to their coming.

The Gestapo did the dirtiest of the dirty work for Hitler.

The SS was the larger organization. At first, the SS was organized to be the personal body guard for Adolph Hitler. Later, SS units were introduced into the regular German army.

The SS were also known for their fanatical fighting on the frontlines. They would stand their ground fighting to the death in hand to hand combat when necessary.

Woven into the SS mode of combat was the almost universal decree from Hitler that troops in the field must fight to the end with no retreat.

The no retreat policy eventually helped bring the war to an end. Hitler ran out of soldiers and had to resort to using young boys and old men to defend Germany.

Hitler with Hitler Youth at the end of the war

Question #16 – Anne Mentions a Ninth Resident in Hiding? Who or What Was It?

#9 - Person, Place Or Thing?

One day, Anne listed each of the Annex residents. She came up with nine. The ninth resident was –

Your choices are:

1. Moortje, the cat.

2. Miep Gies - the sympathetic office employee who came after hours with food.

3. the Weststorm bell tower whose chimes rang on the quarter hour.

4. civility, which was a daily pursuit for everyone.

August 9, 1943

This individual was the most important intermediary between the inside and the outside worlds.

Answer to Question #16 - Anne Mentions a Ninth Resident. Who or What Was It?

Miep Gies 1987

2. Miep Gies - the sympathetic office employee who came after hours with food.

Discussion:

Miep Gies was not Jewish. She would bring food after hours and eat supper with the group.

Miep helped preserve Anne Frank's diary after the war. Miep found the diary after the Annex was discovered by the Nazis.

Later, Miep gave the loose pages of the diary to Anne Frank's father. Miep Gies claimed she did not read the papers.

We are grateful to Miep Gies for having the presence of mind to appreciate and preserve the small bit of order among the chaos.

A moment in time.

One person, one moment, one act made a big difference.

Miep Gies died in 2010 and is listed among the Righteous Gentiles at Yad Vashem Holocaust Memorial Museum in Jerusalem.

August 9, 1943

View into Yad Vashem Memorial Garden

Established in 1953 by the Israeli Parliament, a core principle was to recognize Gentiles who took personal risk without financial or evangelistic motive.

As a consequence of their actions, Jewish brethren were saved. Those recognized were honored by the State of Israel as being the Righteous Among the Nations.

There is a Garden for the Righteous Among the Nations on the grounds of the Yad Vashem Memorial.

Yad Vashem means as a place specifically to memorialize their names and their deeds in order to perpetuate a memory of their names.

The biblical reference text for Yad Vashem may be found in Isaiah 56:4-5.

Question #17 - What Was Anne's View of Sex?

When it came to sex education, sexual experience and marital fidelity, Anne Frank stated –

Your choices are:

1. Premarital purity was a lot of nonsense.

2. It would be particularly damaging for a man to bring prior sexual experience to a marriage.

3. It was best to build one's sexual identity slowly and become informed as thoroughly as possible.

4. It was best for both the wife and the husband to save themselves for marriage and begin the sexual journey together.

Answer to Question #17 - What Was Anne's View of Sex?

1. Premarital purity was a lot of nonsense.

Discussion:

Anne wrote that the reason parents did not inform their children about sex was the parents feared the children would not keep marriage sacred.

Anne felt that it's not wrong for "a man to bring a little experience to a marriage."

Anne's views about sexual anatomy and premarital purity have been edited out of some editions.

March 2, 1944

Question #18 - What Was Margot Frank's View of Peter Van Daan?

After 18 months in hiding, Anne and Peter Van Daan began spending time together. Peter was closer in age to Anne's older sister Margot.

In time, Margot wrote Anne a note expressing –

Your choices are:

1. - that she, Margot, was smart. She was not attracted to a man smarter than her.

2. - that she, Margot, was a little jealous of Anne's blossoming relationship with Peter.

3. - that Anne was intellectually superior to the dull Peter.

4. - that she, Margot, was not close enough to Peter to confide in him even as a friend.

Answer to Question #18 - What Was Margot Frank's View of Peter Van Daan?

Peter Van Daan not Margot's type

Discussion:

When Anne and Peter slipped away to be together, Margot was not that bothered by being left behind. Anne and Margot exchanged some notes on the subject.

Margot was not jealous of Anne and wished Anne and Peter well. Margot felt Peter Van Daan was not intelligent enough for her.

March 20, 1944

MARGOT'S VIEW OF PETER

Question #19 - What Did Anne Tell Peter She Wanted to Be?

When all this hiding was over, Anne Frank hoped to...

What did Anne tell Peter she wanted to be?

Your choices are:

1. become a language teacher.

2. work in a business having lots of authority.

3. become a writer.

4. become a humanitarian in order to pay people back for the help her family received.

Answer to Question #19 - What Did Anne Tell Peter She Wanted to Be?

3. become a writer.

Discussion:

If she could not earn a living as a writer, she planned to write "'in addition to my work."

Little did she know. Anne Frank would become one of the world's most famous writers.

Anne Frank was never able to promote herself or her diary to the world. Nevertheless, her book has gone viral.

May 11, 1944

Question #20 - What Was Anne's View of God?

Although Anne does not mention religion with any frequency or detail, she did make this statement about God.

Your choices are:

1. God seems to have forsaken the Jews.

2. God has nothing to do with the evil they are experiencing.

3. All their prayers would protect the Jews.

4. My life has gotten better. God has not forsaken me and he never will.

Answer to Question #20 - What Was Anne's View of God?

Not to worry - Steadfast

4. My life has gotten better. God has not forsaken me and He never will.

Discussion:

"My life has gotten better. God has not forsaken me and He never will."

- was expressed almost 2 years into the time of hiding and occurred while she was developing a close relationship with Peter Van Daan.

April 11, 1944

Question #21 - What's the Point of War and Why Can't People Live in Peace?

Late in her diary, Anne Frank asks the questions, "What's the point of war?....Why can't people live together peaceably?... Why all this destruction?"

Anne's response was –

Your choices are:

1. There's a destructive urge in people, the urge to rage, murder and kill.

2. War is the work of politicians and business-men.

3. There is a basic goodness in the common man which will rise from the ashes of war.

4. People eventually rebel against war because so much is lost in war.

Answer to Question #21 - What's the Point of War and Why Can't People Live in Peace?

For me (rtu), one of the worst photos of the Holocaust!

1. There's a destructive urge in people, the urge to rage, murder and kill.

Anne did not blame capitalists and politicians.

She thought the common man was "every bit as guilty."

"Until all humanity, without exception, undergoes a metamorphosis, wars will continue to be waged and everything that has been carefully built up, cultivated and grown will be cut down and destroyed, only to start over again."

May 3, 1944

Rachel Rosenberg's aunt had her son shot while the aunt was holding him!

- *in The Holocaust Scream* on Amazon.com

Question # 22 - How Deep Was Anne Frank's Relationship with Peter Van Daan?

A large portion of the second part of the diary concerns Anne's frequent entries about her teenage romance with Peter Van Daan. As for the details from Anne's point of view, it is clear that..

Your choices are:

1. Peter was the initiator. He was Anne's relative and became her close confidant.

2. Peter and Anne were never alone. Their closeness mostly consisted of stolen whisperings.

3. Peter and Anne became close. They openly discussed controversial and adult subjects. There was some physical contact such as kissing and holding hands.

4. Anne is in a teenage romance. Some of Anne's entries during this time are emotionally charged and hard to follow.

Answer to Question # 22 - How Deep Was Anne Frank's Relationship with Peter Van Daan?

3. Peter and Anne became close. They openly discussed controversial and adult subjects. There was some physical contact such as kissing and holding hands.

Discussion:

Anne was the aggressor. At first, Peter Van Daan was shy. In time, Peter and Anne came to share their closely held opinions including their criticism of the others.

Peter and Anne did have time upstairs alone together.

They were not related.

For Anne's part, she had a romantic fire burning for Peter. Anne writes openly about her feelings toward Peter.

There is no suggestion of deep physical involvement. However, we know that Anne had an awakening. She wrote about subjects that were not open for discussion according to the cultural norms of that time.

For example, Anne contemplated her lower female exterior anatomy. So graphic are her verbal illustrations that these portions of her diary have been censored from many later diary editions.

March 2, 1944.

The controversy about her sexual anatomy depictions became a subject for possible censorship in the United States. Should the sexual anatomy text be censored from the diary?

What is your opinion? We would like to know.

Email your thoughts to us at:

theHolocaustScream@cox.net

Question #23 - How Did Anne Feel About Her Hardship & Stress?

DID ANNE EVER LOSE
IT OR BREAK DOWN?

Once she was settled into her hiding routine, Anne Frank expressed her thoughts and feelings.

Anne Frank believed her privations and dangers to be –

Your choices are:

1. robbing Anne of her adolescence and fun.

2. a lot of hardship for an ordinary girl who wanted to be a teacher.

3. every day she was being robbed of a chance to be more mature.

4. a good beginning to an interesting life.

Answer to Question #23 - How Did Anne Feel About Her Hardship & Stress?

The Holocaust perspective: A child's view?

4. a good beginning to an interesting life.

Discussion:

Anne Frank never lost it or broke down.

'What I am experiencing here is a good beginning to an interesting life, and that's the reason, the only reason, why I have to laugh at the humorous side of most dangerous moments.

I am young and have many hidden qualities; I'm young and strong and living through a great adventure; I'm right in the middle of it and can't spend all day complaining because it's impossible to have any fun.

I'm blessed with many things: happiness, a cheerful disposition and strength.

Every day I feel myself maturing, I feel liberation drawing near, I feel the beauty of nature and the goodness of the people around me.

Every day, I think what a fascinating and amusing adventure this is. With all that, why should I despair?"

Question #24 - Why Was Anti-Semitism on the Rise Late in the Nazi Occupation?

Question #24 - Why was anti-Semitism on the rise?

Your choices are:

1. Some Jews gave the names of their Christian helpers to the Germans in response to pressure.

2. The war was wearing out the Dutch Christians.

3. There were bounties of money and goods for those who turned in the Jews.

4. Many Dutch Jews had come from Germany. These German Jews were revealing their German loyalties.

Answer to Question #24 - Why Was Anti-Semitism on the Rise Late in the Nazi Occupation?

"This is true"

1. Some Jews gave the names of their Christian helpers to the Germans in response to pressure.

Discussion:

"This is true."

Anne thought this was understandable. The same would happen if the roles were reversed. It was impossible to remain silent under German torture or threats.

May 22, 1944

Question #25 - What Was Mr. Dussel's Profession?

Mr. Dussel had a particular set of skills

Mr. Dussel was an addition to the original group. He brought a particular skill set to the group. His skills were used. Mr. Dussel was –

Your choices are:

1. Mr. Dussel was a physician.

2. Mr. Dussel was a dentist.

3. Mr. Dussel was an electrician.

4. Mr. Dussel was a banker.

Answer to Question #25 - What Was Mr. Dussel's Profession?

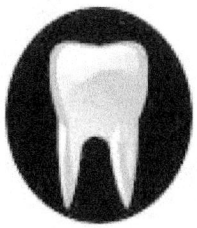

Dentist's object of affection

2. Mr. Dussel was a dentist.

Discussion:

Anne Frank does not refer to Mr. Dussel as Doctor Dussel. That may be the cultural norm as it was in Germany.

Eventually, several of the group needed dental work. Anne reports having a root canal performed without anesthesia!!

Auch.

June 30,1944

Question #26 - Anne Compares Childbirth to What Human Activity?

Anne Frank asserted that "modern women want the right to be completely independent. But that's not all. Women should be respected as well."

In developing her train of thought, Anne Frank proposes that when it comes to childbirth, women should be compared to –

Your choices are:

1. spiritual leaders who shepherd the moral values of the family.

2. teachers every bit as skilled as those teaching school.

3. soldiers and war heroes.

4. hard workers who accept their roles as their destiny.

Answer to Question #26 - Anne Compares Childbirth to What Human Activity?

Female Amazon warrior

3. soldiers and war heroes.

Discussion:

"....in childbirth alone, women commonly suffer more pain misery and illness than any war hero ever does."

Of course, Anne was not writing from experience.

June 13, 1944

Question #27 - How Did Anne Feel About the Easy Life?

Anne Frank believed Peter was inclined to pursue the soft life. Peter had made some comments to that effect. As for Anne and the easy life –

Your choices are:

1. You shouldn't take the easy way out even if it is available.

2. All the people in hiding will need an easy period to recover.

3. After the war, everyone is going to have to find their own way.

4. Easy may be the best or only choice in times of hardship.

Answer to Question #27 - How Did Anne Feel About the Easy Life?

Tell me again – Why is hard work good for me.

1. You shouldn't take the easy way out even if it is available.

Discussion:

"You can't take the easy way out."
You have to earn happiness.

"Earning happiness means doing good and working, not speculating and being lazy. Laziness may look inviting. Only work gives you true satisfaction."

July 6, 1944

Historically, Holland had been a place of refuge for, among others, religious dissidents.

In the prior centuries, Holland had been a center for the Protestant religious movement.

In many of the Dutch Protestant circles, it was believed that hard work was an essential part of the best spiritual existence.

This religious belief in the virtue of hard work may have influenced Anne's ideas.

Question #28 - What Was Anne Frank's Prescription for a Quiet Conscience & Inner Strength?

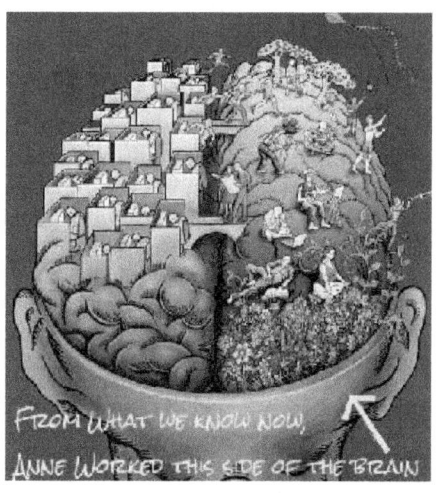

Left brain analytical - Right brain emotional

Anne Frank wrote that she had a free prescription for anyone who "wanted to experience a quiet conscience that gives you strength."

The central idea for acquiring this quiet conscience was –

Your choices are:

1. Don't be so self-centered, opinionated and arrogant.

2. Uphold your own sense of honor and obey your own conscience.

145

3. Do your best to resist evil temptation and bad behavior.

4. Believe in a higher order of things, something bigger than you.

Answer to Question #28 - What Was Anne Frank's Prescription for a Quiet Conscience & Inner Strength?

QUIET CONSCIENCE - INNER STRENGTH

Go to the light!

2. Uphold your own sense of honor and obey your own conscience.

Discussion:

"How noble and good could everyone be if, at the end of each day, they were to review their own behavior and weigh up the rights and wrong. Try to do better at the start of the day...

July 6, 1944

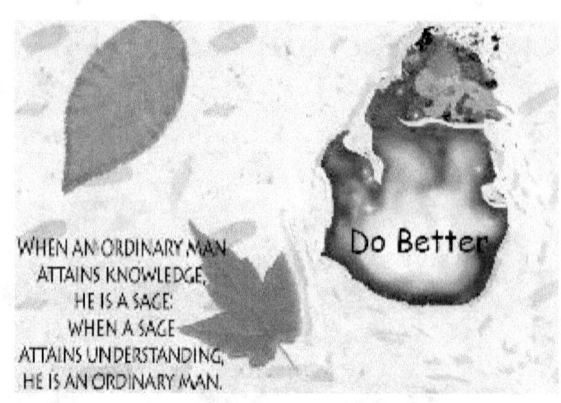

WHEN AN ORDINARY MAN
ATTAINS KNOWLEDGE,
HE IS A SAGE;
WHEN A SAGE
ATTAINS UNDERSTANDING,
HE IS AN ORDINARY MAN.

Do Better

Question #29 - What Was the Meaning of Anne's Last Entry?

Without Warning The Diary Stops - This Bothers Us Even Today

The last entry in Anne Frank's diary states, "If only there were no other people in the world."

Anne Frank feels this way because –

Your choices are:

1. People resent Anne's outspoken nature and attack her.

2. People crowd Anne and cause the bad side of her heart to come out.

3. The other people in hiding were constantly attacking Anne and her ideas.

4. People have an inner drive that causes them to pursue what they want at the expense of others.

Answer to Question #29 - What Was the Meaning of Anne's Last Entry?

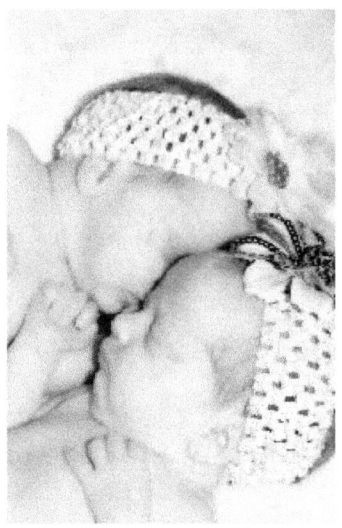

Were there two Annes?

2. People crowd Anne and cause the bad side of her heart to come out.

Discussion:

Anne believed there were 2 Annes. The outer Anne was superficial, flippant, humorous and joyful.

The outer Anne was an enemy to the inner Anne. The inner Anne was finer, better but weaker. The inner Anne was a true friend.

August 1, 1944

Question #30 - How Many Times Did Anne Leave the Annex?

What if you must leave?

The Dutch people were under constant danger from the Germans and their informants. This applied even more to the Dutch Jews.

The streets of Amsterdam were not safe for Jews. Jews could be taken off the streets and never heard from again.

How many times did Anne Frank leave the confines of her hiding place?

Your choices are:

1. 4 times and all for medical reasons.

2. 2 occasions to help carry large quantities of perishable food back to the hiding place.

3. Anne Frank never left her hiding place to go outside.

4. Anne left only one time to get a dental root canal.

Answer to Question #30 - How Many Times Did Anne Leave the Annex?

Zero

3. Anne Frank never left her hiding place to go outside.

Discussion:

There was no doubt in Anne's mind that those in hiding were fortunate. The office women who came almost daily told those in hiding about the roundups of their friends and acquaintances.

There was no illusion about the fate of those rounded up. They were to be murdered. There was no speculation otherwise.

There was no speculation otherwise. Anne was matter of fact about the fate of those lead away which in some cases was at night below her as she looked upon the street from a second story window.

When the group added Mr. Dussel, they were alarmed that he wanted to wait 2 days before he joined them.

Those in hiding thought that any unusual activity on Mr. Dussel's part might alert the authorities.

Nevertheless, Mr. Dussel waited his 2 days.

How about you? Could you stay in the same place for 2 years and be cheerful?

Question #31 - How Old Was Anne Frank When She Was Taken Away?

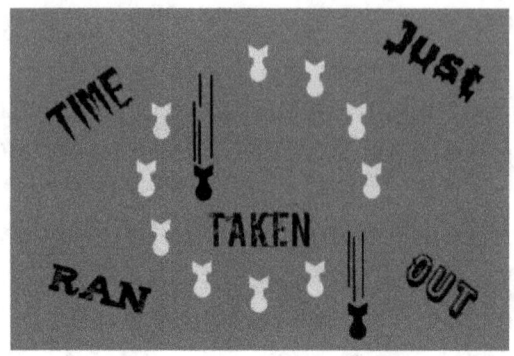

We know from question #15 - Anne Frank knew her fate if caught – Think of everyone's terror!

On August 4, 1944, the Annex was entered by the Germans. How old was Anne Frank when she was taken away?

Your choices are:

1. Age 17.

2. Age 16.

3. Age 15.

4. Age 14.

Answer to Question #31 - How Old Was Anne Frank When She Was Taken Away?

4. Age 14

Discussion:

On August 4, 1944, Anne Frank would have been 8 days from her 15th birthday. According to office workers, the Germans were accompanied by local Nazi sympathizers also known as collaborators.

The captors found more people than they were expecting and had to send for a second car. There apparently was no resistance.

The Annex was sealed shortly afterward as the building was not owned by Mr. Frank.

Question #32 – Do We Know What Happened the Day They Were Discovered?

2. Many of the details of their capture are known including the approximate time of day and the leader of the Germans.

According to reports, the Germans came to the business in the late morning. The Germans went right to the hiding place and took the group captive and led them off.

A German officer by the name of Silberberg led the arresting party. He survived the war but could/would not give many details.

There were no diary entries for that day. The last diary entry had been 3 days prior to their capture. It is thought the group had no warning that the Germans were coming.

Answer to Question #32 - Do We Know What Happened the Day They Were Discovered?

Imagine The Terror

TIME OF THE END

2. Many of the details of their capture are known including the approximate time of day and the leader of the Germans.

According to reports, the Germans came to the business in the late morning. The Germans went right to the hiding place and took the group captive and led them off.

A German officer by the name of Silberberg led the arresting party. He survived the war but could/would not give many details.

There were no diary entries for that day. The last diary entry had been 3 days prior to their capture. It is thought the group had no warning the Germans were coming.

Question #33 - What Did Anne Frank Learn About the Dutch Resistance?

When the Allied armies came into Holland, they found a Dutch resistance movement. Resistance movements against the Nazis were common, especially in the countries west of Germany.

In her book, *The Holocaust Scream*, Rachel Rosenberg describes the resistance movement in Poland as being very weak.

In her six years in the camps, Rachel knew of the resistance movement in Poland but she had no contact with any anti-German partisans.

Returning to Anne Frank,

What did Anne Frank learn about the Dutch Resistance?

Did anyone really resist?

Your choices are:

1. Anne details no specific violent acts by the Dutch resistance.

2. As far as Anne was concerned, Dutch resistance was almost non-existent.

3. The radio reports from the Dutch government in exile always spoke in positive, unrealistic terms about the resistance in Holland.

4. Anne mentions several violent retaliatory acts committed by the Dutch resistance.

Answer to Question #33 - What Did Anne Frank Learn About the Dutch Resistance?

Dutch resistance

1. Anne details no specific violent acts by the Dutch resistance. However, Anne mentions the Dutch church leaders calling for each person to choose weapons and fight for their religion and freedom.

Discussion:

Anne does report bomb damage as a matter of fact. Anne does not criticize the Allies for bombing Holland.

Anne mentions that hostages were taken from the Dutch population and murdered in retaliation for acts against the Germans.

Anne does not relate any overt acts of destruction or assassinations by the Dutch resistance. There were other contemporary reports of some high-ranking German officers and collaborators being killed by the Dutch resistance.

There were methods of soft resistance against the Nazis by the local Dutch authorities and others.

We can imagine some of the methods, criticisms, paperwork issues, fudging on the ration cards etc.

"One good thing has come out of this (high prices and food shortages): As the food gets worse and the decrees more severe, the acts of sabotage are increasing.

The Ration Board, the police, the officials - they are all helping their fellow citizens or denouncing them and sending them off to prison.

"Fortunately, only a small percentage of Dutch people are on the wrong side, writes Anne.

March 29, 1944

In a remarkable letter to their parishioners, the Dutch bishops called for each person to **fight** for the people, country and their religion.

February 27, 1943

The Nazis had hoped to connect to the Dutch because the Germans believed the two cultures were from the same "Germanic stock."

The Nazis believed both peoples were superior and part of the Master Race.

Nazis enter Amsterdam after 10 days of fighting 1940

The Nazis assigned SS units to administer Holland. The SS units were more fanatical than the Wehrmacht or regular army units.

In early 1941, the Dutch staged a widespread solidarity strike to protest the Nazis' treatment of the Jews.

The strike was one of the few public responses to Jewish persecution by any country in Western Europe. The Nazis violently and totally suppressed the strike.

Back in Poland, Rachel Rosenberg found no such conviction to resist the Germans by helping the Jews.

Rachel, at age 14, took it upon herself to ask the priest of the Catholic Church to hide her 3 brothers.

The priest knew the Rosenberg family as Rachel's father had supplied meat to the church. The priest refused out of fear of German retaliation.

In time, Rachel's three brothers were lost in the Holocaust.

What accounts for the overt Dutch resistance?

People do not like to see their country occupied. The Dutch citizens took up the mantle of resistance as their situations allowed.

The exiled government called for resistance as did the church authorities.

In a remarkable letter to the church parishioners, the Dutch bishops called for the people to take up arms and resist in any way they could.

Question #34 - Anne Went Into Captivity with Someone From the Group. Who was it?

Yes or no?

After tracing the fate of each member of the group taken with Anne Frank into captivity, it was discovered that the group had been widely scattered while in captivity.

We do know that Anne was able to have one member of the group accompany her throughout her final sojourn at the hands of the Nazis.

In Anne's case she was accompanied by –

Your choices are:

1. Her father.

2. Her mother.

3. Anne was with the person she liked the least among those in the group, Mrs. Van Daan.

4. Her sister Margot.

Answer to #34 - Anne Went Into Captivity with Someone From the Group. Who was it?

Unfortunately, there are no surviving pictures of Anne's group from the time in hiding.

There are pictures of the major players, including the five key Gentile go-betweens to be found at:

http://www.annefrank.org/en/Subsites/Home/

4. Her sister Margot.

Discussion:

It is true that most of the group were scattered after being captured. However, Anne and Margot spent the final months of their lives together at more than one concentration camp.

They were confined in Germany and Poland.

As far as we know, Margot and Anne were the only ones who kept in close physical contact.

For one thing, the Germans always separated the captives by gender whenever possible.

Question #35 - Who Found the Diary?

Who found the diary?

The diary was found by:

Your choices are:

1. A sympathetic unidentified worker from the first floor of the factory found the diary after the Germans and their captives left the premises.

2. Otto Frank came back and knew where Anne had hidden the book to keep others from reading it.

3. An individual was hired to clean up the mess in the Annex. He found the book and gave it to Miep Gies.

4. Miep Gies, a trusted worker, found the diary scattered on the floor and gave it to Otto Frank upon his return.

Answer to Question #35 - Who Found the Diary?

Miep Gies as seen earlier - a true friend of all in the Annex

4. Miep found the diary scattered on the floor and gave it to Otto Frank upon his return.

Discussion:

Miep Gies was an ever loyal Gentile employee who conveyed necessities and other items to the Annex the whole time the group was in hiding.

Miep would often eat the evening meal with the group. Miep was single at the time.

Not long after the group was captured, Miep found the diary scattered on the floor. She gathered the diary and kept it unread until she was able to give to Otto Frank after the war.

Miep was not taken captive or punished. Miep and her husband survived the war.

Anne never reports any problems with Miep during the time of hiding.

Question #36 What Was the Fate of Anne Frank?

Life or not?

We know that Anne Frank and the others were assembled in Amsterdam at the Westerbork assembly station.

From there they all left Holland.

What happened to Anne Frank after her capture by the Germans?

Your choices are:

1. No one knows for sure.

2. She was murdered in a gas chamber at Auschwitz Concentration Camp.

3. She died of typhus at Bergen-Belsen Concentration Camp.

4. She disappeared into the Auschwitz Concentration Camp. There are no details surrounding her death.

Answer to Question #36 - What Was the Fate of Anne Frank?

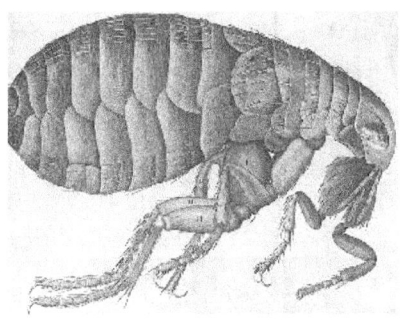

Common flea - Intermediary carrier of the typhus rickettsia infecting agent

3. She died of typhus at Bergen-Belsen concentration camp.

Discussion:

Typhus is an infectious disease caused by a rickettsia bacterium. Fleas are a common carrier of typhus. In all the concentration camps, fleas were a constant worry.

Typhus is known to cause muscular pain, fever, delirium and a total body rash.

Sometimes there would be such severe and extensive typhus outbreaks that the Germans would consider obliterating the camp hosting the typhus outbreak.

After her capture, it was possible to trace Anne Frank's journey through the Nazi camp system.

After her capture, Anne Frank was sent to a holding center in Holland. It was about a month before the first allied forces entered Holland.

From Holland, Anne was sent to Auschwitz for about 6 weeks. From Auschwitz, Anne and her sister Margot were sent back to Germany. They ended up in the Bergen-Belsen Concentration Camp.

Both girls died during a typhus epidemic in early 1945 and are thought to be buried together in a mass grave near what is now Hannover, Germany.

Rachel Rosenberg, a Polish girl who survived 6 years in 4 Nazi concentration camps, reports that she had fleas all the time.

Rachel did bathe in the six years she was confined. Her only course of action was to manually pick the fleas off her body.

Rachel's story is a best seller on Amazon where it is available in ebook and paperback.

Enter the title, "*The Holocaust Scream*" in Amazon search to view Rachel's book.

Be sure to get your copy now while it is fresh in your mind.

Question #37 – What Was the Fate of the Others?

Bristlecone pine living off rocks for thousands of years - a survivor!

Of the eight Jews in hiding, how many survived the war?

Your choices are:

1. None of the eight survived.

2. Otto Frank was the only one who survived.

3. Otto Frank and Peter Van Daan survived

4. Otto Frank and Mr. Van Daan survived.

Answer to Question # 37 - What Was the Fate of the Others?

8 Candles 8 People

Mr. Van Daan (Van Pels) was killed in the Auschwitz gas chambers in late 1944.

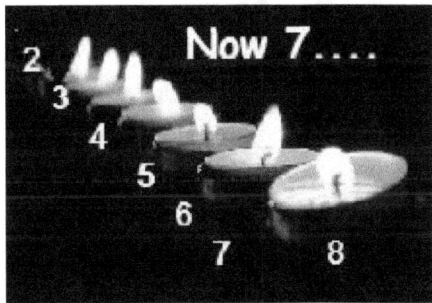

Now 7....

Mrs. Van Daan (Van Pels) was transported to Theresienstadt and was alive until April of 1945.

It is certain Mrs. Van Daan did not survive but the final circumstances of her death are not known.

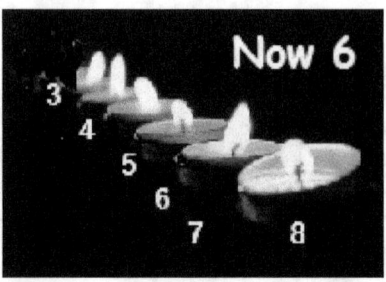

Mr. Dussel (Albert Pfeffer) died on December 20, 1944 in the Neuengamme Concentration Camp.

Edith Frank dies at the Auschwitz Concentration Camp in January of 1945. It is reported that she died of hunger and exhaustion.

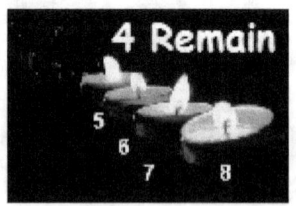

Peter Van Daan(Van Pels) was forced to march from Auschwitz to Mauthausen Concentration Camp in Austria. Peter died in May of 1945, 3 days before the war ended.

Margot Frank and Anne Frank died in Bergen-Belsen Concentration Camp in late February or early March of 1945. There had been an outbreak of typhus.

Anne Frank probably died from typhus. Anne died a few days after her sister, Margot.

Anne Frank's father, Otto, was the lone survivor. He lived until the 1970s and was instrumental in shepherding Anne Frank's story into the world's consciousness.

Question #38 What Percentage of Dutch Jews Were Murdered by the Nazis?

Holland had 140,000 Jews prior to the war.

According to estimates, what percentage of the Dutch Jewish population was murdered by the Germans?

Your choices are:

1. About 30%

2. About 15%

3. About 75%

4. About 50%

Answer to Question #38 - What Percentage of Dutch Jews Were Murdered by the Nazis?

3 out of 4 Dutch Jews were murdered by the Nazis!

3. About 75%

Discussion:

Holland lost 100,000 of its 140,000 Jews. By comparison, Holland's next door neighbor, Belgium, lost about 40%.

It is hard to believe that Germany lost only 25% of its Jews!

There is a country by country listing of the Jews murdered by the Germans here:

http://history1900s.about.com/library/holocaust/bldied.htm

Holland suffered the highest percentage of Jews murdered in the Holocaust!

Question #39 - How Did Holland Relate to Israel During the Oil Embargo of 1973?

After the Arab-Israeli War of 1973, the oil producing Arab states imposed the infamous oil boycott of 1973.

The Arab states were especially upset with the United States for its support of Israel during the just concluded Arab-Israeli War.

The idea was to deny Israel oil and war supplies.

The Arabs characterized a country's help toward Israel as being in one of four groups; pro-Arab, neutral, pro-Israel and uber pro-Israel.

Holland was assigned to which group as a result of its actions during the 1973 Arab-Israeli war?

Your choices are:

1. Holland was placed in the pro-Arab group by the Arabs.

2. Holland was placed in the neutral group by the Arabs.

3. Holland was placed in a special uber pro-Israel group by the Arabs.

4. Holland was placed in the pro- Israel group by the Arabs.

Answer to Question #39 - How Did Holland Relate to Israel During the Oil Embargo of 1973?

Flag of Israel

3. Holland was placed in a special uber pro-Israel group by the Arabs.

Discussion:

Holland remembered.

Not only did Holland join the United States in supporting Israel during the Arab-Israeli War of 1973, but Holland also supplied Israel with oil.

As a consequence, Holland and the United States were assigned to receive even less oil during the embargo than the other pro-Israel offenders who had sided with Israel during the war.

Oil was being rationed. There were those long lines at the gas stations. Gas prices skyrocketed. Gas guzzlers fell out of favor.

I remember the time. Dutch authorities stated they had stood up to the Germans in supporting the Jews in Holland and they would not abandon the Jews in 1973!

At the time, it was a clear statement of principle toward the Jewish people and the state of Israel on the part of Holland and its citizenry.

Do you suppose that part of Anne Frank's legacy was to instill in the people of Holland and abiding loyalty toward the Jews and by extension, to Israel?

#40 - What Was Hitler's Nero Option? Why Was It Relevant to Anne Frank?

1st century Roman coin with image of Nero

Nero was a 1st century Roman emperor. It is said the he set fire to the city of Rome to inflict punishment upon the Romans. It worked.

However, Nero was thought to be mad and was assassinated shortly after Rome was burned.

Likewise, Hitler was mad.

When the Russians were approaching his bunker in Berlin, with only a few days of fighting possible, Hitler ordered his remaining soldiers to systematically destroy the remaining German infrastructure.

His new mantra or spin was to punish the German people for failing Hitler!

Some soldiers followed his orders and began destroying structures that had survived the fighting.

Hitler wanted to make sure all of Germany was in ashes. Hence the connection to Nero.

Relevance to Anne Frank?

While in the grips of the Nazis, Anne and Margot Frank were moved about among several concentration camps.

The mythical Phoenix rising from the ashes every day

Hitler believed that the Germans would find a way to win and like the legendary Phoenix, rise from the ashes of destruction.

This attitude of rising from the ashes has its roots in German warrior mythology which the Nazis embraced like a cult.

Hitler's Nero Option was not something made up at the last minute. Hitler intended to bring the Germans to the lowest point possible so that they would rise to even greater prominence from the ashes - his Phoenix mythological connection.

Hitler had been in a hospital recovering from having been gassed when World War One ended. He was infuriated as to how it played out with the Germans in World War One.

Hitler vowed he would never surrender. Hitler became incapable of surrendering.

As a result, victims in transit like the Frank girls were made to endure the results of Hitler's madness way beyond the point of common sense, practicality or humanity.

Hitler dragged out the war until the Frank sisters were dead in Bergen-Belsen Concentration Camp just weeks before Germany finally surrendered.

Germans soldiers and civilians flooded the roadways trying to get to the West. Still, Hitler held on to the Jewish prisoners.

It had to be personal with Hitler.

By the time the Germans surrendered, Hitler, like Nero was dead.

Hitler wouldn't let go of the Jews like Anne and Margot.

#41 - What About Anne's Controversial References to Her Female Anatomy?

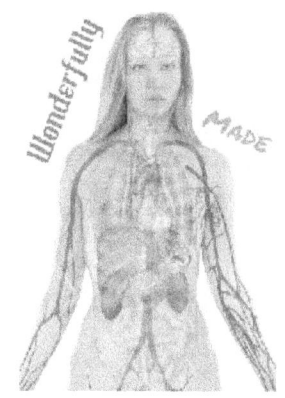

Wonderfully made

You may read what Anne has to say about female anatomy in her entry of:

March 24, 1944

We have a problem and therefore a controversy.

On one hand, we do not want to censor Anne Frank unless perhaps when the work is for a younger audience.

I have written about the Holocaust.

Together with a concentration camp survivor, Rachel Rosenberg, we have written her autobiography, <u>The Holocaust Scream</u>, which is a best seller on Kindle and is available on Amazon in hard copy.

I was convinced to write Rachel's story in her own words without censorship or editing as much as possible.

I even supposed that if Rachel had been involved in a murder, I would tell her story. The Holocaust caused and forced people to do things in the extreme.

Who was I to clean up her story for my personal tastes and sensitivities?

It was not my story.

Please send any comments you might have to:

<u>TheHolocaustScream@cox.net</u>

We hope you have enjoyed the discussion of the book.

Please leave a review on Amazon and be sure to tell others about this remarkable story.

Best wishes for your future.

Robert & Amanda

Addendum: New Information About Mr. Dussel?

Was Anne being fair to Mr. Dussel?

Who was Mr. Dussel aka Dr. Pfeffer**?**

Recent discoveries have brought to light some information regarding Mr. Dussel, the dentist who was Anne Frank's roommate.

Rummaging around some papers, an employee of the Amsterdam Anne Frank Foundation came across some household items belonging to Charlotte Kaletta. Ms. Kaletta was the fianc'e of Mr. Dussel.

The papers were found at an open air Amsterdam flea market. There were a few books and a small box of photographs, including some of the dentist who shared the room with Anne Frank.

The items came to light in 1987, about 42 years after the death of Anne Frank.

While casually viewing the photographs, a figure jumped out at her. Suddenly she saw a portrait of someone she recognized. It was the dentist, Dr. Fritz Pfeffer, called 'Mr. Dussel' by Anne in her diary.

In 1889, Friedrich "Fritz" Pfeffer was born in Giessen, Germany. He trained as a dentist and jaw surgeon. At the age of 22, Dr. Pfeffer obtained his dental certification.

During World War I, Dr. Pfeffer served in the German army. After the war he married and had a son. The couple eventually divorced. Dr. Pfeffer continued to practice dentistry in Berlin, Germany.

In 1936, the doctor and Kaletta met during one of her visits for dental work. Kaletta, whose father was a dentist, was 26 at that time.

Even though the two fell in love, they were unable to marry because of the anti-Semitic Nuremberg laws forbidding interracial marriage.

Anne Frank did not care much for Mr. Dussel.

Anne gives Dr. Pfeffer the pseudonym "Mr. Dussel" (Anne used pseudonyms for many of those in hiding with her.)

In German, Dussel means fool.

Despite Anne's disregard for Dr. Pfeffer, research has shown him to be an active, athletic man who was held in high regard by his community.

He was member of a Jewish rowing club, an accomplished horseman and enjoyed travelling with Kaletta. Dr. Fritz Pfeffer was drawn to the cultures of Italy, Greece and England.

Though persecution laws in Germany barred Jews from public practices, Dr. Pfeffer secretly practiced as a dentist for a dental firm. He worked off the books moonlighting his dental services.

In November 1939, the couple fled to Holland.

The war had started, but Holland was still neutral and not under Nazi occupation. In Amsterdam, the Franks, Dr. Pfeffer and Kaletta ran in the same social circles.

During his confinement with Anne Frank and the others, Kaletta provided Dr. Pfeffer with financial support, toiletries and his dental instruments.

Dr. Pfeffer provided much needed dental care to the other seven Annex inhabitants.

The Rise and Fall of Anne Frank
Can We Prevent It? - Here's How

How do we keep the gripping, compelling and revealing story of Anne Frank in the World's consciousness?

The bigger issue is, how do we keep the Holocaust relevant?

Many if not most issues tend to fade with time. Peoples' interests wander and wane. We move on. That is the way things are.

Some stories develop a life of their own and linger in the public consciousness. Why is that?

How does a story like the Diary of Anne Frank become viral and regenerating?

The answers lie with succeeding generations.

How do we plant the awareness of Anne Frank and the Holocaust in the garden of our children's minds and more importantly, the fertile soil of our children's hearts?

It is easier to keep the Holocaust awareness alive on the analytical side of our consciousness. Despite the Holocaust deniers' emotional efforts, the facts of the Holocaust are well established.

It is on the heart (emotional) side of the issue where we must concentrate our efforts.

This is the key to keeping the memory of Anne Frank and the Holocaust alive and resonating in the hearts of all future generations.

The same applies to Anne Frank's story. There is a reality to her story as well as a gist. Many of us have a working knowledge of Anne's tragedy and the Holocaust.

We know the facts and the flow of the story, but there is more.

But our acknowledgement of the facts is not enough in my opinion, to perpetuate Anne's story.

Here's why.

We need to learn from the Holocaust deniers who take their stand, not on the facts, but rather by doubling down on their emotional understanding.

Their emotions trump the facts, the power of emotion on display.

The Holocaust deniers are not invested in the facts. They shield themselves from the facts.

Typically, the human brain first responds to incoming information in an emotionally loaded way.

The emotional reaction is faster than the analytical response which is measured, deliberate and slow.

In time, the analytical side does come into play.

Gathered facts, associations, peripheral information etc. are tacked on to support and modify the initial emotional reaction, position or impression.

That is, when we allow analysis to influence our brain processes.

For example, we often buy things on emotional impulses. Then we begin to analyze what we have done.

In the process, we see common behaviors such as buyer's regret or doubling down (affirmative support of the decision).

These are two opposite consequences or outcomes. However, they are different sides of the same analytical coin.

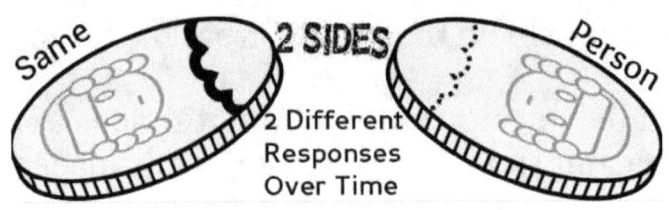

What does this have to do with the Holocaust and Anne Frank's story?

The most powerful way to perpetuate the Holocaust truth is to take the audience or the individual on a journey that involves the emotional side or right side of the brain.

People buy or in this case buy in with their emotions. Again, it's a right brain thing.

Most people get the analytical (factual) side of the Holocaust.

The Holocaust happened and it was bad.

But there is more.

Consider....

I have been telling you about Rachel Rosenberg, a contemporary of Anne Frank and a Holocaust survivor.

Rachel Rosenberg – Holocaust survivor

After years of self-imposed silence, Rachel slowly began to tell her story. In time, she began going to schools. There she would give her witness.

Rachel has spoken to thousands of students, some by satellite from as far away as Hawaii.

Many times the students will send Rachel thank you cards. They are interesting as they reveal illuminating perspectives about Holocaust awareness in our young people.

Let me give some examples of the thank you cards Rachel has received. All are from the same student assembly.

Student thank you note - #1

"Dear Mrs. Rosenberg,

Thanks for coming to my school and telling your story. Hearing your story has made me really realize what happened.

It opened my eyes about how bad it really was.

*You are so nice and it **made me crying** knowing that this happened to you.*

*When you think about your little brother dying I started to crying because **it made me think** about my little brother and what I would do if this happened to him.*

Thank you sincerely, Bonnie"

Rachel's account took Bonnie beyond the facts of the Holocaust. Rachel's story brought Bonnie inside the emotional experience of the Holocaust and made her relate and blossom with emotion.

A very powerful response, as you can see.

I tell Rachel that she is changing lives. Rachel is.

So can you.

Student thank you note - #2

"Dear Mrs. Rosenberg,

Thank you so much for coming to our school. It was very interesting to hear about your personal experience.

I knew about what happened but I couldn't imagine what people were feeling until you came.

It was so nice of you to share your experience with us. Thank you!!!

Sincerely, Amy"

Amy knew what had happened but was taken deeper into her feelings by Rachel.

Student thank you note - #3

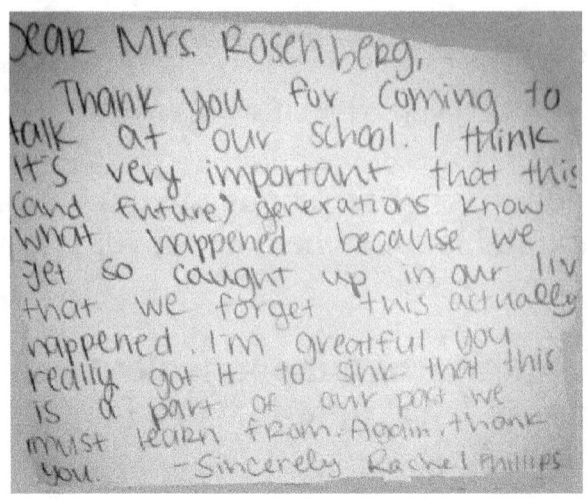

"Dear Mrs. Rosenberg,

Thank you for coming to talk at our school. I think it's very important that this (and future) generations know what happened because we get so caught up in our lives that we forget this actually happened.

I'm greatful you really got it to sink that this is a part of our past we must learn from.

Again thank you.

Sincerely Rachel P"

Rachel P. went on a deep emotional journey through Rachel Rosenberg's account of the Holocaust.

Our Holocaust support should strive to achieve deep emotional responses.

Now you have some tools at your disposal
.

Student thank you note - #4

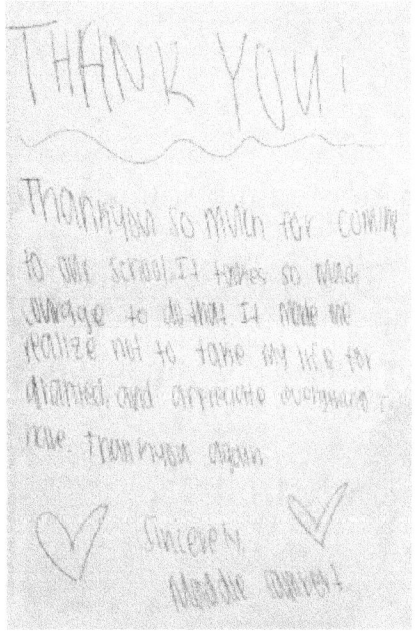

"Thank you!

Thank you so much for coming to our school. It takes so much courage to do that

It made me realize not to take my life for granted and appreciate everything I have. Thank you again

Sincerely, Maddie L."

Maddie L. looked more kindly on her own situation. Something clicked.

This is a common response to Rachel's testimony.

Student thank you note - #5

"Dear Mrs. Rosenberg,

Thank you for coming to our school and telling us about your story.

I don't think anything like this will happen again.

from, Brian"

We still fight for the minds and the future. Brian thinks it won't happen again. What do you think?

The point I want you to see is that we want to avoid Holocaust slippage.

210

Holocaust slippage is the slow steady decline of all things Holocaust into oblivion, disinterest and apathy.

We can't let that happen.

Why, because young Brian is wrong.

It **can** happen again. The Holocaust reveals a fundamental flaw in human nature - mankind can create and collude with evil.

So.... What to do?

Whenever possible, make your Holocaust stand passionate.

Send Holocaust books to people you know and care about. Books like the ones we have discussed, which reveal the passionate side of the Holocaust by touching the reader's emotions.

We have been discussing but three Holocaust books.

You can count on these 3 books to bring out emotional responses.

1. The Definitive Edition: The Diary of a Young Girl - Anne Frank

2. The Anne Frank You Wished You Knew

3. The Holocaust Scream - the story of Holocaust survivor Rachel Rosenberg

There are many more good Holocaust accounts.

Make this list your reliable starter kit for spreading the passionate reality of the Holocaust.

Each of these three books will take the reader on an emotional potentially life-changing journey.

It's up to each of you to take it from here.

Become a keeper of the Holocaust flame.

Keeper of the flame

It's up to you now!

Bibliography & Resources

The authors would like to acknowledge the following resources:

1. Anne Frank, <u>The Diary of a Young Girl.</u> The Definitive Edition. Edited by Otto H. Frank and Marie Pressler. Bantam Books Edition 1997. ISBN: 0-553-57712-3

2. Anne Frank from Cover, <u>Anne Frank History and Quick Study Quiz</u>. Picture of Anne Frank by Wikipedia.com

3. Miep Gies 1987 Wikipedia <u>http://en.wikipedia.org/wiki/Miep Gies</u>

4. Face in Hands by George Hoban. PublicDomainPictures.net <u>http://www.publicdomainpictures.net/view-image.php?image=31241&picture=face-in-hands</u>

5. It's up to you by George Hoban. PublicDomainPictures.net. <u>http://www.publicdomainpictures.net/view-image.php?image=21571&picture=its-up-to-you</u>

6. Anne Frank from Cover, <u>Anne Frank History and Quick Study Quiz</u>. Picture of Anne Frank by Wikipedia.com

7. Rachel Rosenberg. Photograph used with permission from author's personal collection.

8. <u>Hey! You Don't Know Squat About Baseball</u> by Robert and Amanda Urban. Cover used with permission.

9. Anti-Semitism - Flickr files. Public Domain: Anti-Semitism in Berlin, 1933 New York Times Paris Bureau Collection. <u>http://www.flickr.com/photos/pingnews/479872516/</u>

10. Heart from Red Heart. From PublicDomainPictures.net <u>http://www.publicdomainpictures.net/hledej.php?page=240&hleda=love</u>

11. HandcuffISA jpg. From Wikipedia <u>http://en.wikipedia.org/wiki/File:HandcuffISA.JPG</u>

12. Hiding in plain sight from I'm Hiding by Bobbi Jones Jones. PublicDomainPictures.net <u>http://www.google.com/imgres?imgurl=http://www.publicdomainpictures.net/pictures/30000/nahled/im-hiding.jpg&imgrefurl=http://www.publicdomainpictures.net/view-image.php?image%3D22209&h=461&w=615&sz=142&tbnid=01-</u>

SAY-
PCDxHMjM:&tbnh=97&tbnw=129&zoom=1&usg
=_7DRG_4QD5SF9yeQLjNbkeQ1APM0=&doci
d=DpwPeiU4ZLBBbM&itg=1&sa=X&ei=ht9KUq
qXJ8HXygHis4GABQ&ved=0CDQQ9QEwAw

13. Anne Frank House. Wikipedia - The Free En-
cyclopedia http://www.publicdomainpictures.net
/view-image.php?image=25383&picture=happy-
birthday

14. Book Tunnel by Peter Kratoch-
vil. PublicDomainPictures.net http://www.public
domainpictures.net/view-
image.php?image=11604&picture=book-tunnel

15. Father Time Etching from About.com. Con-
tributed by Dixie Allen. Public Domain im-
im-
age http://webclipart.about.com/od/New_Year_
Clip_Art/ss/Vintage-New-Year-Cards_4.htm

16. Happy Birthday. Peter Kratochvil. PublicDo-
mainPictures.net http://www.publicdomainpictu
res.net/view-
image.php?image=25383&picture=happy-
birthday

17. Normal chromosomes. NiH video
2000. http://benchmarks.cancer.gov/nci-b-roll-
collection/cancer-cells-and-genetics/

18. Report Card. Public domain image. http://www.wpclipart.com/education/class work/report_card.png.html

19. Art Poster Public Health Dental Care 1942 - USPHS Vintage Printable. http://www.google.com/imgres?imgurl=http ://vintageprintable.com/wordpress/wp-content/uploads/2010/08/Art-Poster-Public-Health-Dental-care-19421.jpg&imgrefurl=http://vintageprintable.co m/wordpress/vintage-printable-color/color-blue/color-blue-4/art-poster-public-health-dental-care-1942-5/&h=2673&w=2043&sz=526&tbnid=pYivWD5l auhfXM:&tb

20. No German! from Zutritt fuer Unbefugte Verboten by Torsten Henning. Pubic domain. http://www.google.com/imgres?imgurl=ht tp://upload.wikimedia.org/wikipedia/commons/ thumb/0/0f/D-P006_Zutritt_fuer_Unbefugte_verboten.svg/57 5px-D-P006_Zutritt_fuer_Unbefugte_verboten.svg.pn g&imgrefurl=http://commons.wikimedia.org/wi ki/File:D-P006_Zutritt_fuer_Unbefugte_verboten.svg&h =575&w=575&sz=56&tbnid=7taT1tnaodh0AM:& tbnh=90&tbnw=90&zoom=1&usg=__jgn9TGdO Wc3lm7ecW4cT7PjdReo=&docid=YJ0BRFtUUp RpGM&sa=X&ei=3-

9KUvO5FIzyqwGyh4CYBw&ved=0CDQQ9QEwA
w

21. Thumbs Up by George Hodan. PublicDo-
mainPictures.net http://www.publicdomainpictu
res.net/view-
image.php?image=54423&picture=thumbs-up

22. Death in the Hood by George Hodan Pub-
licDomainPictures.net http://www.publicdomain
pictures.net/view-
image.php?image=44608&picture=death-in-the-
hood

23. Miep Gies 1987 Wikipe-
dia http://en.wikipedia.org/wiki/Miep_Gies

24. Romance Silhouette by K Whiteford. Pub-
licDomainPictures.net http://www.publicdomain
pictures.net/view-
image.php?image=37543&picture=romance-
silhouette

25. Public Domain image from Comic Books
Plus. Artist un-
known. http://comicbookplus.com/?dlid=30485

26. Old type writer by Petr Kratochvil. Pub-
licDomainPictures.net http://www.publicdomain
pictures.net/view-
image.php?image=1983&picture=old-typewriter

27. File:Auschwitz Resistance 281.jpg From Wikepedia Commons http://commons.wikimedia.org/wiki/File:Auschwitz_Resistance_281.jp

28. Butterfly - Things will change. From God pictures. Artist unknown. PublicDomainPic-PublicDomainPictures.net http://www.publicdomainpictures.net/hledej.php?page=120&hleda=god

29. Peter - Anne from Children by Karen Arnold. PublicDomainPictures.net http://www.publicdomainpictures.net/view-image.php?image=34593&picture=children

30. Holocaust Monument Moscow by Lynn Greyling. PublicDomainPic-PublicDomainPictures.net http://www.publicdomainpictures.net/view-image.php?image=54473&picture=holocaust-monument-moscow

31. Horse and Rider from PublicDomainPictures.net

32. Dentist from Tooth with blue outline by Jackie Olbina clk-clk-er.com http://www.google.com/imgres?imgurl=http://www.clker.com/cliparts/P/a/i/k/i/M/too

th-with-blue-outline-
md.png&imgrefurl=http://www.clker.com/clipar
t-tooth-with-blue-
out-
line.html&h=297&w=264&sz=20&tbnid=ykkQU
FjqCXKKgM:&tbnh=90&tbnw=80&zoom=1&usg
=   AfX4uOFE8xl4kcimbpoU3XKaGLk=&docid
=S4IO4Fg4P9kjgM&sa=X

33. Aubry Lecomte after Girodet-Trioson 1826
Folio Amazon warrior. Left in the public domain
for research purposes. http://www.albion-
prints.com/aubry-lecomte-after-girodet-trioson-
1826-folio-nude-risque-amazon-warrior-63268-
p.asp

34. Sleep Angel by Piotr Sidleck PublicDomain-
Pictures.net http://www.publicdomainpictures.n
et/view-
image.php?image=41089&picture=sleep-angel

35. Go to the light from Sunshine and Sun Rays
by Maliz Ong PublicDomainPic-
tures.net http://www.publicdomainpictures.net/
view-
image.php?image=31125&picture=sunshine-and-
sun-rays

36. Twins from Twins by Lisa Runnels. Pub-
licDomainPictures.net http://www.publicdomain
pictures.net/view-
image.php?image=45294&picture=twins

37. Zero adapted from Six by Peter Griffin. PublicDomainPictures.net http://www.publicdomain
pictures.net/view-
image.php?image=23453&picture=six

38. The Number 14. Adapted from Number 23 by Eddie Fouse. PublicDomainPic-
tures.net. http://www.publicdomainpictures.net
/view-
image.php?image=22313&picture=number-23

39. Write by Jana Jakeskov Open clipart public domain. http://openclipart.org/detail/2263/write-
by-machovka

40. Dutch resistance adapted from ComicBook-
sPlus.com Author unknown. Public Domain all issues.

41. From Woman Face by Piotr Siedlicki. PublicDomainPictures.net

42. Miep Gies 1987 Wikipe-
dia http://en.wikipedia.org/wiki/Miep_Gies

43. Flag of Israel from Israeli Flag by Marina Shemish. PublicDomainPic-
tures.net http://www.publicdomainpictures.net/
view-image.php?image=15506&picture=israeli-
flag

44. The 1973 oil embargo: its history, motives and consequences.
05/02/2005 http://www.ogj.com/articles/print/volume-103/issue-17/general-interest/the-1973-oil-embargo-its-history-motives-and-consequences.html

45. 3 Out of 4 Murdered adapted from ComicBooksPlus.com public domain comic books

46. How Many Jews Were Murdered? About.com. http://history1900s.about.com/library/holocaust/bldied.htm

47. Common flea from Wikepedia.com

48. Six by Peter Griffin. PublicDomainPictures.net http://www.publicdomainpictures.net/view-image.php?image=23453&picture=six

49. 8 Candles from Candles by George Hodan. PublicDomainPictures.net http://www.publicdomainpictures.net/view-image.php?image=36780&picture=candles

50. Kitty from Old Community by Randal Lee. PublicDomainImages.net http://www.publicdomainpictures.net/view-image.php?image=25691&picture=old-community

51.Quote from Simon Wiesenthal, Stichting, Anne Frank (20 September 2005). "Reaction decease Simon Wiesenthal, WieAnne Frank House. Archived October 2012.

52. Anderson, Anthony E. (1995). Anne Frank was not alone: Holland and the Holocaust [Online]. Available: http://www-lib.usc.edu/~anthonya/holo.htm [1995, October 24].

53. Father Tried To Get Anne Frank to the U.S. Amy Clark CBS News AP February 14, 2007. http://www.cbsnews.com/news/father-tried-to-get-anne-frank-to-us/

54. In addition, the authors would like to thank and acknowledge that 37 images were taken from the public domain on the Internet.